SPECTACLE IN THE ROMAN WORLD

Classical World Series

Classical World Series

SPECTACLE IN
THE ROMAN WORLD

Hazel Dodge

Bristol Classical Press

First published in 2011 by
Bristol Classical Press
an imprint of
Bloomsbury Academic
Bloomsbury Publishing Plc
50 Bedford Square
London WC1B 3DP
&
175 Fifth Avenue,
New York, NY 10010, USA

CIP records for this book are available from the
British Library and the Library of Congress

ISBN 978-1-85399-696-2

Illustration sources and credits
Figs 1, 2, 5, 6, 7, 11, 12, 13, 15, 16, 18, 21 and 25: photographs by
Hazel Dodge. Figs 3, 4, 8, 9, 10, 14, 17, 22, 23, 24, 26, 28, 29, 30, 31:
drawings by M.C. Bishop. Fig. 19: after K. Coleman, 'Fatal Charades:
Roman Executions staged as Mythological Enactments', *Journal of
Roman Studies* 80 (1990), 44-73, reproduced by kind permission of
the Roman Society and Professor Coleman. Fig. 20: reconstruction
of Augustus' stagnum in Rome according to Rabun Taylor,
reproduced by kind permission of Professor R. Taylor.

Typeset by Ray Davies
Printed and bound in Great Britain by
CPI Antony Rowe, Chippenham and Eastbourne

www.bloomsburyacademic.com

Contents

Acknowledgements

I would like to thank the several generations of Trinity College Dublin undergraduate students who have chosen to take my Entertainment and Spectacle course in their final year; they challenged my thinking and made me re-evaluate my ideas on several occasions. I am also very grateful to my colleagues in the Department of Classics, Trinity College Dublin, for many fruitful 'spectacular' discussions, and I would particularly like to acknowledge the generous support of the Centre for Mediterranean and Near Eastern Studies. My particular thanks go to Professor Kathleen Coleman and the Roman Society, and Professor Rabun Taylor for their permission to reproduce their reconstructions of Augustus' *stagnum*. I am very grateful to Dr M.C. Bishop for his drawing expertise; most of the line drawings, unless otherwise acknowledged, are his exceptional work. Deborah Blake at Bristol Classical Press has proved she has patience beyond measure and I acknowledge with gratitude her support throughout. My warmest thanks to you all.

I am forever grateful to my parents for their tremendous encouragement in all my endeavours. My greatest debt of gratitude goes to my husband, Jon, who has always been constant in his love, support and academic companionship, and who read the text rather more times than he expected! I dedicate this to you.

Note on Sources, Spelling and Abbreviations

For ancient place-names I have used the Latin spelling as being the more familiar to a modern reader.

For literary sources, I have given references to the original ancient works, with the titles translated into the most commonly used form in English wherever possible. For inscriptions I have given the *CIL*, followed by volume number and inscription number, or *ILS* number. For coins I have given the *RIC* number.

BMC = British Museum Catalogue = Coins of the Roman Empire in the British Museum.
CIL = Corpus Inscriptionum Latinarum, 1863-.
ILS = Inscriptiones Latinae Selectae, 1892-.
RIC = Roman Imperial Coinage, 10 volumes, London 1923-1994.

Chapter 1

Approaching Roman Spectacle

'*Panem et circenses*', bread and circuses, were the two things for which, according to the satirist Juvenal, the Roman mob yearned. The supply of food to the masses in Rome was always a political issue as well as a life-giving one. Rome flirted with famine, and in the later Republic this became a powerful bargaining chip in the constant political negotiations between politicians and voters. In the same way, public spectacles, the origins of which lay in religious festivals and the honouring of the dead, became a powerful mode of communication with Rome's population. They also became a potent symbol of Rome's place in the world. The plethora of buildings for public entertainment which survive across the empire stand as testament to its importance in Roman society generally, and to the willingness on the part of the emperors and local elites to provide fitting venues for a range of displays.

The study of Roman spectacle has long fascinated modern scholars and the general public alike, and it presents controversial and disturbing challenges to a modern understanding of the Roman world. However, new research and major discoveries are providing new insights into the subject and encouraging radical re-evaluation of some of our long-held views. Aside from the entertainment buildings themselves, the evidence available for the study of Roman spectacle is rich and geographically varied. It would also be a mistake to assume that provision of spectacles at Rome was the same as across the empire, or that there were not very significant regional variations.

Archaeological evidence

Very few entertainment buildings have been fully excavated and properly published. This is unsurprising considering the size of such structures, but it has meant that their interpretation is often problematic. The venues themselves provide the largest and most obvious evidence for Roman spectacle, and there have been some exciting new discoveries in this area in the last two decades. For example, an amphitheatre was finally identified and excavated in the late 1980s and 1990s in London. In 2004, the first known circus in Roman Britain was discovered at Colchester. The identification in 2006 of the amphitheatre at Sofia (ancient Serdica) in Bulgaria has made another addition to the increasing list of amphitheatres in the eastern part of the empire, further emphasising that the Greek East enjoyed Roman spectacles as much as other regions of the Roman world. At Caesarea Maritima on the coast of Israel, excavations over the last 20 years in the area between Herod's summer palace and the harbour have uncovered an entertainment building, termed an 'amphitheatre' in the historical sources, yet which takes the form of a stadium with starting gates and a central barrier for horse and chariot racing. Most importantly, it has highlighted the necessity for scholarly flexibility in interpreting the form and function of entertainment buildings as well as in the terminology employed in their discussion.

Finance for the construction of spectacle buildings came from a variety of sources, but from the late Republic such facilities, and the entertainments associated with them, were being identified as appropriate vehicles for self-advancement by prominent figures. There are many examples of this phenomenon, and the financial input could vary. The whole practice is encapsulated in the construction of the theatre at Dougga (northern Tunisia) under Marcus Aurelius. Publius Marcus Quadratus, who had served in Rome as a judge and held various offices in the nearby Roman colony of Carthage, was keen to provide for his home town; it was a good opportunity to advertise his own career success. The inscription recording this act for posterity was placed on the stage building:

> Publius Marcus Quadratus, son of Quintus, of the Arnensis tribe, priest of the imperial cult, pontiff of Colonia Iulia Carthago, called to the 5 decuriae [of judges] by the emperor Antoninus Pius, Augustus, built for his homeland using his own funds, in accordance with being flamen, a theatre, from the foundations, with basilicas, a portico, *xystoi*, a stage building with curtains and the greatest ornamentation, and at the occasion of the dedication, staged dramas, distributed hand-outs, provided a public feast and gymnastic displays. (C. Poissot, *Les Ruines de Dougga*, Tunis 1983)

Modern scholars define Roman entertainment buildings in very distinct architectural terms and assign apparently clearly categorised functions. However, some structures had a very long history and were adapted over time as culture and society evolved. There was also wide variation in the provision and form of these facilities across the empire. A further factor is the terminology used for these buildings. The term 'amphitheatre' (*amphitheatron*: Greek for 'seating on all sides') for the elliptical structure which comes to be associated in particular with gladiatorial displays was not commonly used until the first century AD when the building type itself became more physically defined. The earliest datable permanent amphitheatre is at Pompeii, and in the dedicatory inscription (*CIL* 10.852, 70-65 BC) it is called a '*spectacula*', a word usually used for the entertainments themselves. Many terms are similar in both Greek and Latin and therefore pretty much interchangeable without any misunderstanding. However, this is not the case with the Latin 'circus' and Greek 'hippodrome'. They mean essentially the same thing, a venue for various types of equestrian events, in particular chariot racing, but there is a modern tendency to use one for the Latin West and the other for the Greek East as if they indicate two different types of building.

Literary sources

Literary evidence is particularly important for the Republic, a period for which there is less physical evidence, and often provides the context for specific types of display. However, the bias is very much towards spectacles staged in the city of Rome, and there was almost certainly an emphasis on the really important and lavish displays; the written sources are far less informative about entertainments in the wider Roman world. Indeed, there must have been many much smaller events in Rome itself that just did not make it into the headlines, let alone elsewhere in the provinces.

There are several literary works which provide more detailed accounts of aspects of Roman spectacle. For example, the first book of Martial's epigrams, often referred to as the *Book on Spectacles* (*Liber Spectaculorum or Liber de Spectaculis*), seems to have commemorated Titus' inauguration of the Flavian Amphitheatre, the Colosseum, in AD 80. The associated games lasted for 100 days and included not only gladiators and chariot races, but also staged battles and executions, all for the delectation of the crowd and the glory of the emperor. In his work of poetry, Martial aimed to provide a glowing account of the emperor and his generosity. As such, although a tremendously valuable source, the work cannot be taken as an accurate, historical account.

Tertullian's work, *On Spectacles* (*De Spectaculis*), provides a Christian commentary on Roman spectacle in the late second/early third century AD. He found little to favour, and for the modern scholar the work's great worth is in its incidental references and the information that can be gleaned as Tertullian rages against pagan idolatry.

Legal sources provide much valuable information on contemporary attitudes to the performers themselves. Roman society was driven by

1. Ephesus. Tombstone of the gladiator whose name can
be translated as Black Cyril, with victor's palm branch.

social status, and thus loss of status, for any reason, meant being considered outside society with the loss of a number of public rights. This was
infamia, originally something suffered by an individual as a result of their
own wrong-doing, and it would be recorded in the census register of
citizens. By the end of the second century BC, anyone who had fought in
the arena or appeared on the stage was tainted with *infamia*, creating
the paradox that is so clear in the context of gladiators: such people
provided important social activities, and came to be much acclaimed
and celebrated by the crowd, yet were also viewed with contempt by
society as a whole.

Epigraphic evidence

There is a wealth of epigraphic evidence that supplies further information. Tombstones, for example, can provide the names of performers, their career details, their life-span and some indication of access to wealth; the choice to set up a tombstone was an expensive business for the deceased's estate or heirs (Fig. 1). Other epigraphic material gives details of the games staged, those responsible for them (the *editor*), and sometimes even including detailed costings. There are also records from gladiatorial schools (*ludi*) which supply details of individual names and fighting styles, as well as a record of a gladiator's career. Less formal in nature is the invaluable material represented by the graffiti from Pompeii, sometimes accompanied by scratched images (see Figs 9 and 10). Painted posters advertising future attractions often gave details of the different 'acts', and in several cases attracted spectators by the promise of awnings (*vela* or *velaria*) to shade the audience from the sun. An important group records the outcome of individual fights (sometimes accompanied by a visual record), while others allow insights into spectator attitudes. For example, a Thracian gladiator, Celadus, was the subject of a number of scribblings, and in many of them he was described as a 'girl's heart-throb'; another, Crescens, was described as the 'Netter of young girls by night', presumably a pun on his fighting style as a *retiarius* (*CIL* 4.4342, 4.4345).

Iconographic evidence

Iconographic evidence relating to Roman spectacle is immensely varied in media and rich in detail, ranging from mosaics and wall-paintings to sculptural reliefs (sometimes accompanied by inscriptions) and representations on coins, lamps and pots. When taken together, these provide a surprisingly accurate visual record of dress, equipment and weaponry, fighting styles and the range of animals involved, as well as the physical environment of the spectacles. Mosaics such as the Zliten mosaic from the Villa Dar Buc Ammera near Lepcis Magna (Libya) (Fig. 2) and the Villa Borghese mosaic from Rome are reminders that Roman spectacle was not a simple affair, that going to the games meant a programme of varied visual spectacles (for the audience), keen appreciation of the performers' skills, and marvellous exotic beasts.

Reconstruction and re-enactment

Unsurprisingly, the recent rise in popularity of historical re-enactment has also embraced Roman spectacle. Such work, based on the archaeological and iconographic evidence, allows practical testing of current theories. Obviously not all elements can be simulated, such as animal fights and

2. *Opus sectile* and mosaic floor from the Villa Dar Buc Ammera,
Zliten, near Lepcis Magna (Libya).

executions, but many other aspects of these displays can be explored.
Notably Marcus Junkelmann, a German re-enactor, after being involved
in the reconstruction of Roman military equipment for many years, turned
to exploring the equipment and fighting styles of different gladiators.
Even if some scholars do not agree with all his interpretations, this kind
of work helps to provide the evidence with a physicality that would
otherwise be lacking. Equally, in the area of circus racing, reconstructions
of the chariots have provided greater understanding of the practicalities
of races and the differences between Greek and Roman forms. Even
Hollywood has played a part in this process, albeit often with a skewed
view, creating its own 'Roman' culture.

Scientific study

The recovery of human remains from individuals who took part in Roman spectacles is extremely rare. Some skeletons from excavations in London, Rome, Trier in Germany and Patras in Greece have been identified as those of arena fighters, but the evidence raises major doubts. In 1993, a spectacular find of a gladiator-graveyard was made at Ephesus in Turkey, identified by the conjunction of burials with gladiatorial gravestones. The subsequent scientific study of the associated human individuals has challenged long-held views and expanded knowledge, particularly concerning fighting styles, training, dietary regimes and elements of social community.

Chapter 2

The Circus and Chariot Racing

Equestrian sports in Greece and Etruria

Chariot racing was one of the most popular sports in the Greek and Roman worlds; more importantly, it was the one that enjoyed the greatest longevity. In the Archaic, Classical and Hellenistic periods, racing on horseback was popular with the Greeks as well as the usual two- and four-horse chariot races; however, although horse racing continued into the Roman period, other than in the eastern part of the empire it never found as much favour as the racing of chariots.

The earliest description of a chariot race can be found in Homer's *Iliad* (23.287-650) in the context of the funeral games of Patroclus. Here a group of heroes competed against each other in four-horse chariots on a flat plain which served as an improvised race course. They raced in an anti-clockwise direction with only one turning post; there were no starting gates and they drew lots to determine their starting position, clearly a key factor in their success or failure. This is how chariot and horse racing effectively took place before the Roman period, with no monumental, purpose-built venue or elaborate facilties provided. The only pre-Roman hippodrome for which we have any evidence with regard to form is that at Olympia; Pausanias described an *aphesis*, a set of starting gates (*Description of Greece* 6.20.10-15). He made no mention of the number of chariots it accommodated, but he says that each side was 400 feet in length. The mechanism to start the race was set into an altar and seems to have been quite a spectacle in its own right, causing the statue of an eagle to jump up, while that of a dolphin dived downwards; the competitors then set off stall by stall. The whole process would have raised the pre-race tension as well as increasing the spectacle.

Chariot racing and other equestrian events were equally popular in Etruria, to judge from sixth-century BC tomb frescoes and vase paintings. Two-horse chariots (*bigae*) are depicted, as well as horse racing, but there is also evidence for special three-horse chariots (*trigae*). While chariot racing remained important in Rome, horseback-racing was never prominent, except in very specific religious contexts. For example, in March, the Equirria took place on the Campus Martius; this was a festival of horse racing traditionally started by Romulus in honour of Mars. Another equine contest, the Ludus or Lusus Troia, an obscure and very ancient event held in the Circus Maximus, involved a parade of highborn youths on horseback in armour who carried out various complicated manoeuvres, a kind of equestrian military tattoo. The most important contest for chariot racing, however, was the Ludi Romani, held in honour of Jupiter and dating back to the foundation of the Republic.

According to Strabo (*Geography* 5.3.8), the extraordinary size of the Campus Martius permitted it to accommodate not only chariot races but also every other type of equestrian event. However, the main venue for chariot racing in the city was the Circus Maximus, though it did not begin to acquire any kind of monumental facilties until the late Republic. By this time the circus as a building type had taken the shape of a hairpin and was the largest class of entertainment building, used first and foremost for chariot races, although it was the venue for other types of spectacle as well. In their canonical and monumental form circuses were a later architectural development than theatres and amphitheatres, although the spectacles for which they served as venues have a much longer history.

Although the Circus Maximus was the largest and most prominent location for chariot racing in Rome, there were other structures and areas which were used for equestrian displays. A rather ambiguous one was the Circus Flaminius, an area established in 220 BC in the southern part of the Campus Martius by Gaius Flaminius Nepos, champion of the people. This never adopted the shape and facilities of a circus, but remained an open piazza. Horse racing took place here on occasion, for example, the Ludi Taurii, the Taurian or Tarentine Games, were held there every five years on the occasion of the census. Caligula constructed a circus on the slopes of the Vatican Hill, which was further monumentalised by Nero. Both these emperors were fanatical supporters of the circus, and this was essentially a private venue, built so that the two emperors could practise their driving skills. Caligula had placed an Egyptian obelisk on the central barrier of this building where it stood until it was moved in the late sixteenth century to become the central focus of the Piazza San Pietro. This circus was almost certainly the site of the execution of St Peter. Circuses were favoured locations for spectacles of judicial execution.

The Circus Maximus in Rome
The largest of all Roman circuses was the Circus Maximus in Rome, situated in the valley between the Palatine and the Aventine Hills. Traditionally, it was the Tarquins who developed this area for equestrian events; it was the location of many cults and the oldest recorded games,

the Consualia, associated with the rape of the Sabine Women, which were held by Romulus at the altar of Consus near the far turning post. For a long time the structure was fairly insubstantial, resembling the Greek hippodrome, with seating either directly on the hill slopes or in the form of timber bleachers. There were no proper starting gates until 329 BC (Livy 8.20.2); their form and how they functioned is unknown. It was probably not until the early second century BC that the circus started to acquire other more definite facilities. The central barrier at this time took on a more permanent form with turning posts (*metae*) at both ends, each consisting of three adjacent markers. In 174 BC the first of two sets of lap counters was provided in the form of seven eggs, each one presumably lowered as each lap was completed (Livy 41.27.6). These were refurbished in the late first century BC by Agrippa, who also provided a second set in the form of dolphins (Dio 49.43.2), apparently because mistakes were being made in counting the laps.

By the time of Augustus the central barrier or *spina* was also adorned with a number of statues and trophies in addition to the lap counters. Most of these do not survive and the details of their appearance and relative locations are supplied only by literary and artistic evidence. Two monuments do survive, two Egyptian obelisks, although they have since been moved from their original location. They were found and recorded in the fifteenth and sixteenth centuries where they had fallen on the spina. The first obelisk, originally set up at Heliopolis by Ramses II in the thirteenth century BC, was erected by Augustus in 10 BC and now stands in the Piazza del Popolo. This set a pattern for obelisks in circuses in Rome and around the Roman world, for example in the Vatican Circus and the Circus of Maxentius in Rome, and at Tyre, Caesarea Maritima, and Constantinople in the east. In AD 357 Constantius II followed Augustus by erecting a second obelisk with hieroglyphs of Tuthmosis II (fifteenth century BC) in the Circus Maximus; this now stands in Piazza San Giovanni in Laterano. Other monuments on the central barrier included fountains and water basins, a number of towers, statues on columns, and statuary groups, the most important of which was Cybele riding on the back of a lion.

Julius Caesar had carried out some modifications, providing the lowest tier of seating in stone and adding a channel (*euripus*), 3 metres wide, which separated the track from the spectators; and Claudius rebuilt the *carceres* in marble. However, it was not until the reign of Trajan that the biggest transformation occurred (see Fig. 29). The whole building was given a monumental aspect with increased seating and massive supporting substructures of brick-faced concrete at the curved east end (*sphendone*). To commemorate this event, a number of coins were issued with an angled

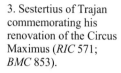

3. Sestertius of Trajan commemorating his renovation of the Circus Maximus (*RIC* 571; *BMC* 853).

bird's-eye view on the reverse so that both the interior and the exterior are visible (Fig. 3). The form of the circus is very clear, with an arcuated exterior façade. The central barrier and its monuments are also visible, including the turning posts, the lap-counters and the Augustan obelisk. By this time the overall length of the building was about 600 metres (track length about 540 metres) with a width of 150 metres. Modern estimates of seating capacity vary from 150,000 to 350,000, with the latter quite credible for the Trajanic building. Along the northern side of the circus, on the slopes of the Palatine, Augustus built the *pulvinar*, a sort of imperial box. This was a sacred area reserved for those presiding over the games and is clearly depicted with a hexastyle façade with a pediment on a mosaic found at Luni in Northern Italy.

Chariot racing at Rome

The development of chariot racing was very closely connected with the physical development of the main venue. Chariots raced in multiples of four and never more than twelve, the number which could be accommodated by the *carceres*. Already by the second century BC there is evidence for stables owned by prominent individuals which trained and provided horses and charioteers for the circus. From the principate of Augustus to the twelfth century AD, four factions, or professional stables (*factiones*), are attested, each team identified by its own colours: white worn by the Albata, red by the Russata, blue by the Veneta and green by the Prasina. Domitian added a further two, gold (Chrusa) and purple (Purphyria) (Dio 67.4.4), but they were short-lived. Where any imperial favour was shown it was usually towards the Greens or Blues. The Reds were often paired with the Greens and the Whites with the Blues, and by the sixth century the organisation of chariot racing had become so thoroughly institution-alised that the Blues and Greens were considered the major factions. This pairing may have stemmed from a particular type of race, the *diversium*, in which the winner from an earlier race would swap teams with the driver from a related faction. Such a test of skill guaranteed added excitement and enjoyment for the crowd, and even greater acclamation for the successful charioteer. By the time of Augustus, the circus games had become big business. The *factiones* were essentially companies under the emperor's patronage, which supplied teams to the magistrates giving the games and generated revenue from prize-money. The stables (*stabulae*) for each of these teams were located in the Campus Martius.

For the staff of the *stabulae* an inscription from the time of Domitian (*ILS* 5313) gives the structure of the *familia quadrigaria* of Titus Ateius Capito of the Red team, one of several groups of that colour. Capito was the faction master, a Roman citizen of high status, and other individuals of the *familia* are mentioned by name and function. A certain Docimus is named as the overseer and Chrestus as the *conditor*, presumably responsible for establishing the stables. At least six charioteers are mentioned by name. Then there was the *tentor* (actually three individuals apparently performed this function) who operated the starting gates; the *morator* who held the horses within the starting gate; the *sparsor* who threw water at the horses to keep them cool while they raced; and the *hortator* who rode on a horse either behind or in front of the chariot giving encouragement and advice on the best course to take (Fig. 4). There was also a doctor and a blacksmith. In addition, there must also have been coaches, trainers and grooms.

The number of races in one day presumably depended on the context of the games and who was funding them, but in Rome it may have been as many as 24 (Dio 60.23.5; 27.2), emphasising again the high level of organisation required. A day would start with a procession into the Circus which would include the charioteers and a chest for sacred objects (*tensa*). Even though by the imperial period many of the spectacles of Rome had become much more secular in context, their religious origins were never completely lost. The procession would be cheered by the crowd and would give the spectators an opportunity to check out the competitors and decide on their bets. A trumpet would blow to draw the attention of the crowd and the presiding magistrate would signal the start of the race by dropping a napkin (*mappa*) (see Fig. 5). When the starting gates flew open the race had begun (see Fig. 6). The *carceres* were placed on a curve, effectively creating a staggered start. The chariots sprinted in straight lines towards the break line at the first turning post and were not allowed to cut across each other. The chariots raced anti-clockwise completing seven circuits of the central barrier; the finish line was halfway down the track just before

4. Campana plaque depicting a charioteer approaching the *metae* (turning posts). The mounted figure to the right is presumably a *hortator*, whose job was to scout out the best route for the charioteer to steer.

the far turning-post, in exactly the same position as the finish line on a modern athletics track. The race therefore was at least 3 miles (5.2 km), in length, requiring huge stamina and strength on the part of both the horses and the charioteers. The race would have lasted a thrilling eight minutes with speeds of up to 45 miles an hour on the straight. To overtake on the inside as one approached the turn was a tactic particularly admired, because it was extremely dangerous! Interestingly, the chariot race in the most famous film version of *Ben Hur* (USA 1959), which for all its inaccuracies and flaws, managed to capture the tension, excitement and dangers of the sport perfectly, lasts 8 minutes and 20 seconds, giving a very good idea of a Roman spectator's experience. Crashes were extremely common, particularly at the start and the turning posts, as the charioteers tried to make sharp and tight turns at high speeds. These are a staple of both literary and visual circus imagery. A particularly detailed account of a race in which the charioteer named Consentius claimed an exciting victory by coming up from behind can be found in a fifth-century AD poem by Sidonius Apollinaris (*Poems* 23.323-424*)*.

In the intervals between the races it was important to keep the crowd entertained, and it became the practice to stage other types of spectacle in the Circus for this purpose. Novelty races might be staged to add variety.

Teams of up to ten horses, for example, might be used, or there might be exhibitions of trick-riding. The *desultores*, attested in 169 BC (Livy 44.9.3) rode two horses reined together, jumping from one to the other. They are also mentioned by Suetonius (*Julius* 39.2) in the context of Caesar's extensive games and spectacles of 46 BC, during which unusually high-ranking young men were the performers. It was in this context of interval entertainment that athletic displays were staged for the first time in Rome in 186 BC, as part of the games of Marcus Fulvius Nobilior (Livy 39.22.1-2), which also saw the first wild beast displays. A sixth-century AD circus programme on a papyrus found at Oxyrhynchus in Egypt (*POxy.* 2707), one of only three extant examples, lists mimes, athletic displays, a hunt, and singing rope-dancers, the latter obviously very popular as they appeared twice. At the end of the games, the victors received a victor's palm, crowns and other prizes (Fig. 5).

The charioteers
In Greek contexts charioteers were aristocratic in status, but this gradually changed, and by the Roman period they were drawn from the lower social classes, freedmen and slaves. As with gladiators, those who were success-ful could achieve major celebrity status, being idolised by the public. Some were able to earn enough in prize money to retire as wealthy men. In many of the inscriptions relating to chariot racing, the names of charioteers often indicate a mix of nationalities, though many have Greek, but few Roman names. A particularly successful charioteer was Gaius Appuleius Diocles who came from Lusitania (*CIL* 6.10048). In his career spanning 24 years he appeared in 4,257 races, winning 1,462. He drove for three different factions, indicating that at least by the second century AD charioteers could be free agents, rather like modern jockeys. As well as mentioning single-entry races, involving competition between four chariots, one drawn from each faction, and double entry races, involving two from each, this inscription also attests triple entry races, where three chariots from each faction took part. They acted as a team and the point was to have one of them cross the line first; the rest wreaked havoc among their opponents. A number of general observations can be made from this inscription. It specifically mentions that 110 of Diocles' first-place fin-ishes were in the opening race; this was obviously a major and signal event to win. The races with larger fields were not considered the premium events; spectators wanted to see champions racing each other. Diocles won 815 races leading from the start, emphasising the importance of gaining the poll position in the initial sprint. Rarely did a charioteer win from behind, although Diocles managed it in the final stretch 502 times. He is also described as having made nine horses hundred-race winners,

and one horse a two-hundred-race winner, indicating that horses could achieve fame just as the charioteers did (many are named in artworks). Diocles' career winnings came to a total of 35,863,120 *sestertii*, estimated somewhere in the region of £1.5-2 million. He died at the age of 42, having enjoyed a lengthy career of 24 years. A number of other charioteers are known from their tombstones, and although they were clearly successful, none achieved the heights of Diocles apart from Porphyrius in Constantinople in the late fifth/early sixth century AD.

Circus mosaics
Circus and chariot racing was a favoured theme in Roman art, appearing on sarcophagi and in mosaics. The circus was a popular motif for mosaics in the western provinces and North Africa, and a number of very fine examples survive from the late third and early fourth centuries (Figs 5 and 6). They depict a race in progress, at all stages, in remarkable detail, and provide the best evidence for the appearance of the central barrier of a Roman circus. Some of these provincial mosaics, it has been argued, reflect the arrangement of the Circus Maximus in Rome. The two most informative examples are the pavement at the villa of Piazza Armerina on Sicily (Fig. 5), and the Barcelona circus mosaic.

5. Great Circus Mosaic, Piazza Armerina (Sicily). Victorious charioteer including the trumpeter, important at both the start and end of the race to get the crowd's attention.

6. Circus Mosaic, Silin (Libya). Detail of the starting gates.

The mosaic at Piazza Armerina depicts the chariots racing anti-clock-wise around the central barrier, with the starting gates at the right-hand end. Behind the gates, several drivers are shown preparing to race. At the left-hand end, spectators are sustained by a youth carrying loaves of bread on a tray (an example of early fast food). The central barrier monuments most likely reflect the arrangement in the Circus Maximus. Among several colonnaded pavilions, there is an obelisk, a statue of Magna Mater on horseback and the lap-counters in the form of eggs, showing three still raised. A crash has occurred at the far turning post, and in the upper part of the mosaic the victor, wearing a green tunic, is being declared and presented with a palm-branch.

The Barcelona mosaic is similar in overall design, although the details on the central barrier are better preserved. Four charioteers are shown, each representing one of the four stables (Reds, Greens, Blues and Whites). The Blue team has crashed and the Green team is victorious. There are two further figures shown near the right-hand turn; one carries a small *amphora* and is probably a *sparsor*, intent on cooling the horses with water. The other figure seems to be waving a piece of cloth, although his function is rather obscure. A particularly noteworthy feature of the mosaic is that the horses are named in inscriptions, whereas the chari-oteers are not. It has been suggested that the owner of the house in which this mosaic was laid was involved in the breeding and training of horses, for which Spain was famous in the Roman world.

Circuses and chariot racing in the Roman empire

As a result of their vast size none of the many circuses in the Roman world has been completely excavated. Compared to amphitheatres and theatres they are relatively rare, were generally provided at a later date (second century onwards) and marked a city out from others as a centre of power. One of the best-preserved and most thoroughly investigated is at Lepcis Magna in modern Libya. The structure lay outside the city limits next to the shoreline. To the south was an amphitheatre built in AD 56, and when the circus was completed in the mid-second century AD the two were connected by open passages and tunnels carved through the hillside. The unification of these two entertainment buildings in a single architectural complex is unparalleled elsewhere in the Roman world. The arena of the circus was almost exactly 450 metres in length, making it one of the longest after the Circus Maximus in Rome. The starting gates were placed along a shallow arc so that all the chariots had the same distance to travel to the near turning-post. The good preservation of the starting gates at Lepcis Magna is unique and sufficient to allow reconstruction of the opening mechanism by which the races were started. An attendant pulled a lever that activated a catapult system, which in turn jerked out the latches of the gates of each stall, allowing the gates to fly open. It is assumed that something similar would have been provided in the Circus Maximus.

Over a dozen circuses are physically known in the Iberian Peninsula. Two particularly well-preserved examples can be found at Mérida in the south-west and at Tarragona on the north-eastern Mediterranean coast. Both are second-century in date, but they differ in terms of location. The circus at Mérida is located outside the walls, while at Tarragona the circus was built on a terrace very much within the urban centre in association with the Temple of the Imperial Cult. Recent work has identified much of the substructure to the seating preserved in the lower storeys of later buildings. The curved end has been cleared of modern buildings and is now open to view. The position of this circus emphasises the important ideological connection between Roman spectacle and the imperial cult. In 2004 the first circus to be identified in Britain was found at Colchester.

In the East, where equestrian events were already well-established, monumental circuses do not appear as uniformly as in the West. A number of eastern cities are known to have had chariot racing at one period or another, but fewer cities are known to have possessed a large monumental circus, and these tend to be major Roman cultural and administrative centres.

There were essentially two types of circus structure built in the region, The larger type of building (such as Tyre in Lebanon, Antioch-on-the-Orontes in south-east Turkey and Bostra in southern Syria) had close similarities with circuses built in the West in terms of overall proportions. The smaller type (for example at Jerash in Jordan, Corinth in Greece and Caesarea Maritima in Israel, all three excavated and published in the last two decades) were much shorter at about 300 metres. It seems to have been a development and reflection of the complex cultural mix of the eastern Mediterranean, one which was intended to be multifunctional from the outset or was later modified to accommodate other types of spectacle. Very few monumental circuses have been identified in Greece and Asia Minor. At Anazarbus in Cilicia (southern Turkey), an unexcavated circus is still visible outside the city walls. It was 410 metres long, 64 metres wide, and had a central barrier. The circus at Thessaloniki in northern Greece was built as part of the Tetrarchic palace by Galerius, an indication of the important relationship in later antiquity between imperial palace and circus, a relationship which had been established in Rome between the Palatine palaces and the Circus Maximus, and was later emulated at the late Roman capitals of Constantinople, Sirmium (Serbia) and Milan.

This lack of monumental circuses may perhaps be explained by a continued preference for Greek-style horse and chariot racing at a local level, which did not require the scale of facilities demanded by Roman-style racing.

Chapter 3
Gladiators and Gladiatorial Displays

In modern public perception gladiators and gladiatorial display are characteristically Roman, summing up Roman culture as militaristic, bloodthirsty, cruel and uncivilised in its attitudes towards human life. However, such a perception ignores or misunderstands the reasons behind the extraordinary public success that gladiatorial displays came to enjoy. They not only had an important cultural function but also played a very significant political role.

Gladiatorial origins
The origins of gladiatorial combat are obscure and continue to be hotly debated by modern scholars. The evidence does not fit neatly together, but two main lines of argument have crystallised. The older view, first suggested in the middle of the nineteenth century, is that gladiatorial games originated in Etruria and were passed on to the Romans along with a number of other cultural traits (a view proposed by a number of ancient writers, e.g. Nicolaus of Damascus, *Ath.* 4.153-4). The second theory, first proposed in the early twentieth century, attributed gladiatorial origins to the Osco-Samnite cultures of Southern Italy. The literary evidence is contradictory, and the origins of gladiatorial combat were contentious even in ancient times. The physical evidence is rich and varied, consisting of the physical structures which housed gladiatorial displays, inscriptions, artifactual and forensic evidence, and iconographical representations. The range of media involved in the last in particular points to a certain familiarity and connoisseurship amongst the viewing public.

A number of Etruscan tomb paintings at Tarquinia (Italy) of the sixth century BC have been identified as depicting gladiatorial combat, for example the Tomb of the Bigae and the Tomb of the Augurs. Helmeted men, sometimes wearing a cuirass and armed with a shield and a sword are shown in rather static poses, but never actually in combat. It has been suggested that they may have been performers in the Pyrrhica, a showy kind of military parade involving flashy military manoeuvres, rather than combatants locked in some kind of bloody conflict. A possible Etruscan origin of the term for the trainer of gladiators (*lanista*) has also recently

7. Fresco from Tomb 53, Andriuolo necropolis, Lucania.

been questioned, and it is by no means certain that the mallet-carrying figure called Iovis Frater by Tertullian (*Ad Nationes* 1.10.47), whose job it was to remove the corpses of dead gladiators from the arena, should be associated with the similarly accoutred Etruscan god Charun.

The material evidence from Southern Italy is much more explicit. Scenes of single combat are depicted in Lucanian tomb paintings dating to the later fourth century BC in the area around Paestum (for example Tomb 53 in the Andriuolo necropolis, and Tomb 10 in the Laghetto necropolis). As well as scenes of chariot racing and boxing matches, men armed with shields, sometimes wearing helmets and carrying spears, are shown fighting each other. That real combat is shown is clear from the amount of blood visible in a number of them (Fig. 7). These seem to be representations of combat as public entertainment within a funerary context, a phenomenon well known in the classical world and beautifully exemplified by the funeral games of Patroclus in Book 23 of Homer's *Iliad*. According to Livy (9.40.17), gladiatorial combat was also part of the entertainment at Campanian banquets.

The first historically documented presentation of gladiators, three pairs drawn from prisoners of war, took place in 264 BC in the Forum Boarium in Rome, part of a gift display (*munus*) staged by Marcus and Decimus Brutus in honour of their father Decimus Junius Brutus Pera (Livy, *Periochae* 16). The sources are silent on whether the combat was to the death, but the connection between gladiatorial display and funerals as well as warfare is very clear. In 216 BC, in honour of Marcus Aemilius Lepidus, his three sons staged gladiatorial displays over a period of three days, involving 22 pairs of gladiators in the Forum Romanum, the usual location for such events during the remainder of the Republic (Livy 23.30). Over the next two centuries the scale and frequency of gladiatorial shows steadily increased; they were still staged within a funerary context, but became an increasingly significant part of more general aristocratic status display, a factor made more important as imperial resources grew through conquest. However, it should be remembered that because of the nature of the sources, we only really hear of those displays that were out of the ordinary for their day.

By the middle of the first century BC, although the funerary context was still evident, gladiatorial displays had become a powerful tool in the struggles between prominent politicians intent on gaining and maintaining popularity and influence. Thus in 65 BC, when he was *aedile*, Julius Caesar gave elaborate funeral games for his father involving some 320 pairs of gladiators. His father had died 21 years before, but Caesar was in dire need of support at Rome and he was prepared to bankrupt himself, borrowing hugely from Crassus, in order to acquire it (Plutarch, *Caesar* 5).

The gladiators
The connection between *munera* and warfare becomes increasingly clear into the late Republic, emphasised by the fact that the gladiators themselves were often prisoners of war forced to fight at the funerals of Roman generals who had defeated their home territories. Some of the main gladiatorial types were named after some of Rome's main enemies, such as the Samnites, Gauls and Thracians. By the imperial period gladiatorial ranks had broadened to include:

- condemned criminals, sentenced to fight in the arena (*ad ludum damnati*);
- prisoners of war, far fewer in number than in the last two centuries BC;
- slaves, some of whom were bought by trainers (*lanistae*) from dissatisfied owners who looked upon this as a form of punishment, a practice finally banned by Hadrian;
- free gladiators (*auctorati*). These were individuals who voluntarily signed up with a *lanista* for a fixed duration, usually five years. It was possible to earn a respectable sum for retirement if a man survived the

arena, but, as with convicted criminals, once released from service their *infamia* debarred them from future public office.

The early combats presumably ended in the death of one of the combatants in each pairing, but as gladiators became big business, this was far less common. It took years to train a good gladiator; thus very few contests between trained gladiators were to the death. Some scholars have suggested that death was the result of as many as 50% of all combats, but most now agree that the figure should be much lower, at 5-10%. It was possible for a gladiator to gain great popularity and wealth and retire very comfortably on the proceeds. Although gladiators, along with actors and charioteers, were considered *infames*, i.e. they had very low status, they were very much admired by the public for their skill. Rather like modern Spanish bullfighters, display of skill, as well as military *virtus*, by the combatants was part of the enjoyment of the spectacle for the spectators, although there was also the enticing possibility of the shedding of human blood to add an extra *frisson* to the occasion.

There is a certain amount of literary evidence for an enrolment oath taken by those voluntarily becoming gladiators, similar to the *sacramentum* taken by soldiers on enlistment (Seneca, *Letters* 37). Petronius (*Satyricon* 117.5) recorded the oath, which he rendered in an exaggerated style, as follows:

> We solemnly swear to obey (the *lanista*) in everything. To endure burning, imprisonment, flogging and even death by the sword.

The phrase, 'Those who are about to die salute you' (*morituri te salutant*), apparently uttered by gladiators before combat and made so famous by Hollywood depictions of the arena, is actually a popular myth. It occurs once in Latin literature, in Suetonius' account of Claudius' staged naval battle on the Fucine Lake in AD 52 (*Claudius* 21), and was actually the words of condemned prisoners manning the galleys.

Types of gladiator
The names of twenty or so different types of gladiators are known from literary and epigraphic sources, but few can be described in detail. 'Gladiator' literally means a man who fights with a sword, but the term came to refer to someone who fought in the arena against another person in single combat, no matter how he was armed. From the second century BC gladiators were trained in specific fighting styles and they would usually be paired with an opponent who was differently armed.

This was a further test of skill, while maintaining the fairness of the fight, and introduced an element of unpredictability to the outcome. All gladiators had some kind of dagger, which could be used for the final killing blow, and many wore helmets. Artistic evidence, such as the Tiber Relief (see Fig. 8), indicates that until the early first century AD these helmets did not have visors to provide protection to the face or a measure of anonymity.

The earliest attested gladiators are the Samnite, the Gaul, and the Thracian. The Samnites and the Gauls were Rome's traditional enemies of the mid-Republic. All were originally lightly armed, reflecting the native fighting style, but by the first century AD all were heavily armed with a shield and arm and leg protection; the torso was left bare.

Samnite/*hoplomachus*. The Samnite was probably originally a light-armed gladiator fighting in the Samnite fashion with shield and spear; by the end of the Republic he was one of the standard heavily armed gladiators. At the beginning of the imperial period he was known as the *hoplomachus* (Greek for 'heavily armed fighter'), probably because it was felt inappropriate to equate an Italian with the indignity of the arena. He wore a large crested helmet with a visor, and a thigh-length greave on his left leg. He is sometimes shown with a large rectangular shield of the type used by legionaries, but he was more often equipped with a small round shield, hence the need for protection on his left leg. He was armed with a long spear and a short dagger. The *hoplomachus* usually fought against either the *murmillo* or the Thracian, both heavily, but differently, armed gladiators.

Gaul/*murmillo*. The Gaul, like the Samnite, was probably originally lightly armed using the traditional Gallic weapons: a long flat shield with a spindle boss and a cut-and-thrust sword with a straight blade about 60 centimetres long. By the late Republic he was armed with a slashing sword and had acquired a helmet, a short greave on his left leg, and segmental arm protection (*manicae*) on his sword arm. He carried a large oblong curving shield. At the beginning of the imperial period, the Gaul, just like the Samnite, underwent a change of name, to *murmillo*, derived from the Greek word for the fish (*murmuros*) which decorated his helmet.

Thracian (*Thraex*). The Thracian first appeared in the arena in the second century BC when Thrace (roughly equivalent to Bulgaria) first came into contact with Rome. Armed with a broad-brimmed helmet, a relatively small, usually rectangular shield, and two thigh-length greaves, the Thracian is recognisable in the iconography by the distinctive shape of his weapon, the native Danubian curved short sword (*sica*) (see Fig.

26). This was a particularly vicious weapon that could efficiently rip open flesh, causing very significant bleeding. The Thracian was renowned for his speed and dexterity, and usually fought the *murmillo* or the *hoplomachus*.

Secutor. The *secutor* ('pursuer') is the most easily identified of the gladiatorial swordsmen. He was armed with the curved rectangular legionary shield (*scutum*) and sword (*gladius*) and usually wore a segmental arm-guard (*manica*) on his sword arm. His smooth, egg-shaped helmet with simple metal crest and no brim was unique and appears to have been specially designed so that it would not be caught in the net of the *secutor*'s main opponent, the *retiarius*. Such an enclosed helmet must have significantly impaired the gladiator's sight and hearing, not to mention his ability to breathe. However, it also gave the wearer a rather sinister appearance, contrasting with the unprotected head of his most usual opponent, the *retiarius*.

Retiarius. The *retiarius* or net man (from the Latin *rete*, net) is probably the most famous of the gladiator types, although strictly speaking, as he did not use a sword, he should not be described as a 'gladiator' at all. The *retiarius* was very lightly armed and therefore could move swiftly and easily, providing a good balance and contrast to the fighting style of the *secutor*. He had no head protection and wore only defensive armour on his left arm with an upstanding plate (*galerus*) affording some protection to face and shoulder. Some artistic depictions show armour covered the left side of the torso as well. The *retiarius* would lead with his left and could tuck his chin into his left shoulder, thus reducing the area of the head as a target. His main weapons were those of a fisherman: the net and the trident. He also carried a dagger. The long trident allowed the *retiarius* to keep a safe distance from his opponent, who had to avoid being caught in his net and then finished off by his dagger, while he tried to slash the exposed arm or legs or stab at the torso of the *retiarius*. The pitting of the swift-footed *retiarius* against the much slower moving, heavily armoured *secutor* could produce very exciting connoisseur bouts and came to be the most popular combination in gladiatorial shows.

Contraretiarius and **arbelas-gladiator.** This type of gladiator seems to have fought specifically against the *retiarius*. He is attested in epigraphic evidence (as *contraretiarius*) from the western empire (e.g. *CIL* 6.631; 33983, both from Rome), although we have no depiction to identify specific weaponry. Indeed, it may be that this was an alternative name for the *secutor*. However, a type of gladiator is attested artistically in the eastern empire, equipped with a half-moon shaped knife (Greek *arbêlas*) attached to an armguard which fitted onto the left arm, admirably suited to cut through the net of the *retiarius*; he also wore a helmet similar to that worn by a *secutor*, and carried a dagger or short sword. He seems to have worn a thigh-length cuirass of scale-armour (although some modern scholars identify it as quilted).

Two types of gladiator which are less well-known, both of which fight their own type, are the *provocator* (plural *provocatores*) and the *eques* (plural *equites*).

Provocator ('challenger'). This type of gladiator has attracted little attention among modern scholars, but he does appear in a number of artistic depictions, for example the Tiber Relief (see Fig. 8). The *provocator* typically wore a masked helmet often with feathers on either side, carried a large shield that was rectangular or a cut-off oval shape, and was armed with a sword. On the lower left leg he wore a greave and his lower right arm was protected by *manicae*. The most distinctive element of the *provocator* was the rectangular chest-plate, the *cardiophylax*, which was held in place on his upper chest by leather straps. No other gladiator wore protective armour on the torso.

Eques ('horseman'). The *equites* are mostly shown in artistic depictions on foot, but in fact (as their name implies) they were horsemen on white horses (Isidore of Seville, *Origins* 18.53). They usually fought the opening bouts in a day's programme and can be seen at the beginning of the procession on a funerary relief from Pompeii and now in the Naples Museum. Later in the same frieze they are fighting on foot. They would start off on horseback armed with spears and carrying round shields, as shown on a stucco relief, the 'Tomb of Umbricius' outside the Herculaneum Gate at Pompeii, but would dismount to end the bout using swords. Their helmets were a simple but distinctive bowler-hat shape with a wide brim and mask and decorated with feathers; they are depicted in a number of mosaics, in particular the Zliten mosaic from North Africa and a mosaic now in Madrid but found on the Via Appia in Rome.

The Tiber Relief (Fig. 8)

A sculpted panel found in the River Tiber between Rome and Ostia and dated to between 30 and 10 BC gives a number of insights into contemporary gladiatorial combat. Three combatants involved in two bouts are shown. An inscription running along the top of the relief gives the professional record of each gladiator and the outcome of the particular fight. On the left are two gladiators; they each wear a helmet with feathers on either side, a heavily folded loincloth with a broad metal belt, and an over-the-knee greave on their left leg. They are equipped with a sword

8. The Tiber Relief, 30-10 BC.

and large rectangular shield with rounded corners, and their right forearms
are protected by *manicae*. The breastplates on their upper chests identify
them as *provocatores*. The inscription above the left-hand figure reads
IVL VVV (*Iulianus pugnarum V coronarum V, vicit*), which identifies
him as a member of the *ludus Iulianus*, a prominent gladiatorial school of
the early imperial period, originally founded by Julius Caesar at Capua.
This was his fifth fight and in all five he had been awarded a *corona*, a
victor's laurel wreath bestowed not just for victory, but also for outstand-
ing feats of arms. Most importantly, he was the victor in this bout also.
The poses of the figures also clearly indicate his victory; his opponent,
Clemens, has his arm raised and has dropped his shield, both iconographic
shorthand for a gladiator's surrender. The inscription records that he was
reprieved (M, *missus*) and allowed to leave the arena alive. *Missio* was
granted to gladiators who, although defeated, were deemed to have fought
bravely. To the right of the relief is another fight, but the slab is broken
and only one opponent is clearly depicted. He is different from the other
two. His torso is bare and he wears a helmet with flowing crest and is
probably a *murmillo*. His large shield is lowered and his sword is lowered
and dropping to the ground. His pose indicates that he also is defeated and
the letters MΘ to the right of his head that he received *missio* but later died
of his wounds. (The Θ, standing for *thanatos*, 'death' in Greek, is the *theta
nigra*, the black theta indicating death in the arena.) Of his victorious
opponent only a small rectangular shield can be discerned and an over-
the-knee greave, but he may have been a Thracian. One further important

point is that none of the gladiators on this relief have enclosed helmets with face-masks. Face-plates for gladiatorial helmets are only really found from the later Augustan period onward. It has been suggested that this was to de-personalise the wearer for both his opponent and the audience, but protection would have been a much more important consideration; bloody face wounds may have disrupted the bout in the way that sometimes happens in boxing matches.

Gladiatorial armour from Pompeii

The largest body of surviving gladiatorial equipment was discovered in 1766/7 in the excavations of the portico attached to the theatre at Pompeii which at the time of the eruption of Vesuvius was serving as a gladiatorial barracks. Most pieces are now in the National Archaeological Museum of Naples. Among the finds were fifteen gladiator helmets, of which eleven had lavish embossed decoration and all were intended to have face-plates; six single short greaves; one single medium-length greave; five pairs of long over-the-knee greaves; three shoulder guards; and a small round shield. The helmets in particular are very ornate and include in their embossed decoration scenes from the arena and allusions to military victory. The decoration is so elaborate that it has caused some scholars to suggest that this equipment could only have been used for the parade (*pompa*) at the beginning of a day's games. There is no identifiable damage on the equipment and, it is claimed, it is too heavy for actual use. However, the elaborate and showy decoration is exactly what is needed in the arena; display, not just of fighting skills, but also of equipment is an important part of the *spectacula*. The embossed decoration in copper alloy also served to increase defence through corrugation. The swords, which are stabbing weapons, are quite light but would have caused damage to unprotected parts of body; but it was important for the bout to last so that the spectators could enjoy the display of fighting skills between two differently armed but evenly matched opponents, not to be over in a matter of minutes. In fact it was only the trident of the *retiarius* that could do ferocious damage through armour, and as result the *secutor*'s helmet was thicker than other gladiatorial head protection.

The fact that some parts of the body were armoured and others left unprotected called for specialised fencing styles. It might be thought that leaving the torso bare, the case for nearly all gladiators, would lead to an inevitably short fight, but this does not take into account the visual stimulation of rippling muscles so often referred to in the ancient sources.

Training

Gladiatorial training was closely related to military training methods. At the end of the second century BC the consul Publius Rutilius had employed *lanistae* to train his legionaries using the same methods they used to school gladiators. As fighting displays increased in public significance, so it was important to have a ready supply of fit and skilled gladiators. Gladiatorial training schools (*ludi*) run by *lanistae* are known from the second century BC; such schools are first attested at Capua in Campania and were owned by wealthy Roman aristocratic families. In the late Republic there was a lively trade in gladiators, for example Lentulus Batiatus (Vatia), the nobleman owner of the *ludus* to which Spartacus belonged, was a *speculator* in gladiators for the personal troupes (*familiae*) of members of the Roman aristocracy. Atticus bought a troupe of trained gladiators as a financial investment in 56 BC, which was repaid after just two matches (Cicero, *Atticus* 4.49.2; 8.2). In 49 BC Julius Caesar established his own *ludus* at Capua. In Rome there were four imperial gladiatorial training schools, all probably established by the time of Domitian if not before, the *Ludus Magnus*, *Ludus Dacicus*, *Ludus Gallicus* and *Ludus Matutinus*. All were in the vicinity of the Colosseum and the last was for the training of beast fighters (*venatores*) (see Chapter 4). A procurator of equestrian rank, appointed directly by the emperor, was in charge of each school, which had a full staff of armourers, trainers and doctors. There were up to 2,000 gladiators accommodated in these schools in Rome. Part of the Ludus Magnus, the largest and most important of the training establishments, was situated just metres east of the Colosseum (and connected to it by a tunnel); its full plan is preserved on the *Forma Urbis Romae*, but part of the building can still be seen. This took the form of an oval arena about three-quarters of the size of the Colosseum arena, surrounded by rooms on a number of levels; a small bank of seats allowed for about 3,000 spectators, and an opportunity for Roman matrons to experience, at close quarters, the rippling muscles of gladiators, which according to the literary sources, provided such a draw for them. Privately owned *ludi* and gladiatorial *familiae* were not allowed in the city of Rome but clearly existed elsewhere in the empire, and the *lanista* of the school could either hire out gladiators or stage games himself.

By the later first century AD a rank structure for gladiators had emerged, giving clear evidence of the highly organised nature of the training. The novice (*novicus*) was a new arrival at the *ludus*; the *tiro* was the recruit who was felt ready for his first fight; having survived his first fight, the gladiator was termed *veteranus*. The gladiator would train initially using a double-weight shield and wooden sword striking at an upright stake (*palus*) set in the ground to become proficient in methodology and to build up stamina. Only when he had gained proficiency against the stake and his worst errors had been eliminated, would he begin using proper weapons against a chosen adversary.

Gladiatorial graffiti from Pompeii

As well as the best surviving examples of gladiatorial equipment, Pompeii has also preserved a large amount of graffiti, including some pictorial examples, relating to gladiatorial shows and the form of the gladiators themselves. Some of these are advertisements for upcoming spectacles, for example:

> 20 pairs of gladiators of Decimus Lucretius Satrius Valens, perpet-ual priest of Nero and 10 pairs of gladiators of Decimus Lucretius Valens, his son, will fight at Pompeii on 8, 9, 10, 11, 12 April. There will be a regular hunt and awnings. Aemilius Celer wrote this on his own by the light of the moon. (*CIL* 4.3884, dated to after AD 50: Pompeii III.vi.2)

Other graffiti are rather like form cards, naming the gladiators, giving their previous record and the outcome of their most recent combat. A particularly interesting series, with accompanying pictures, was found on a tomb outside the Porta Nuceria. Some refer to a gladiator, Marcus Attilius (Fig. 9). In his first fight, as a *tiro* (*CIL* 4.10238a), he was successful against the veteran fighter Hilarus of the Neronian school, who had won thirteen out of his fourteen previous bouts. Presumably because of his conduct in this particular fight, as well as his track record, Hilarus was granted *missio*; he lived to fight another day. In his next fight, which was in a set of games at nearby Nola, Hilarus was victorious (*CIL* 4.10237). Attilius' next fight was against another veteran fighter, Lucius Raecius Felix, and also ended in success for him and a reprieve for his opponent (*CIL* 4.10236a) (Fig. 9). This graffito illustrates an interest-ing convention in gladiatorial iconography; the defeated gladiator is shown falling to his knee, swordless and helmetless, the shield held at an angle so as to be totally useless. This can be seen in a number of other artistic representations, including the Tiber Relief and the Zliten mosaic. Another graffito (*CIL* 4.8056) appears to show a left-handed gladiator, Albanus, a southpaw in boxing parlance, very definitely dominating his opponent (Fig. 10).

9. Graffiti from Tomb 14EN in the Nuceria Gate necropolis, Pompeii, detailing the first two combats of the career of Marcus Attilius. *Above*: 'Marcus Attilius, novice, victor; Hilarus, Neronian, fought 14, 12 victories, reprieved' (*CIL* 4.10238a). *Below*: 'Marcus Attilius, fought 1, 1 victory, victor. Lucius Raecius Felix, fought 12, won 12, reprieved' (*CIL* 4.10236a).

10. Graffito from Pompeii showing a left-handed (*scaeva*) gladiator. It reads 'Severus, ex-slave, 13 victories reprieved(?). Albanus ex-slave, left-hander 19 victories, won' (*CIL* 4. 8056).

Gladiators at Ephesus

In 1993 an amazing archaeological discovery was made in excavations outside the east end of the stadium at Ephesus (Turkey): that of the only securely identified gladiator graveyard. Three gladiatorial gravestones were found *in situ*, all dating to the turn of the second to third century AD; a fourth tombstone belonged to a female slave. The human remains from this cemetary comprised several thousand bones and bone fragments, and the cemetery had clearly been in use over a long period of time. Forensic studies have shown that at least sixty-eight individuals were represented; all but two were male between the ages of 20 and 30 who had died from wounds received in combat. A number of injuries were ante mortem and had healed. From the examples of acute trauma, the head was the most frequently damaged area, followed by the torso. This is particularly interesting given that most gladiators appear to have worn helmets; indeed, the neck muscles of these Ephesus gladiators were highly developed, suggesting the regular wearing of a heavy helmet. Perhaps the men's helmets were removed at some stage during the fight, probably for the *coup de grâce*. One particular head wound was caused by a trident and demonstrated that the central prong of the weapon was barbed.

From the shape and size of the bones it is quite clear that the training was harsh and intensive, the enlarged bones indicating heavy muscular development. There is also evidence for the kind of sports injuries we know of from modern athletes, but it is evident that the training was properly monitored; there are no stress fractures which would occur from overly harsh regimes and medical care for broken bones was very good. The skeletons also give information on the diet of the gladiators which was high in carbohydrates such as vegetables and pulses, particularly barley and beans. Interestingly, according to Pliny (*Natural History* 18.4), gladiators were called 'barleymen' (*hordearii*), presumably because that grain formed an important part of their diet. Foods such as these would have allowed the gladiators to develop a layer of fat which would have provided some protection against body blows and minor cuts. However, weapons such as the Thracian *sica* could still cause horrific wounds and major enervation through blood loss.

Women and gladiatorial display

Female gladiators (*gladiatrices*) were far less common than their male counterparts; the evidence for them is sparse and often ambiguous, but they did exist and their rarity gave them extra popularity with the audience. A senatorial decree of AD 11 laid down a minimum age for freeborn individuals before they could sign up as a gladiator or act on the stage, 25 years for men and 20 years for women. A few years later further legislation forbade upper-class women from becoming gladiators; it appears that they had been unable to resist the lure of the arena. Evidence suggests that women fought Amazon-style with one breast bared, emphasising their totally un-Roman female behaviour – and making them even more attractive to the Roman male. Both Martial (*Epigrams* 6.6.7) and Juvenal (*Satires* 6.251-67) poke fun at the butch nature and over-developed physiques of female gladiators, emphasising how out of the ordinary such fighters were considered to be by the Romans. Tacitus (*Annals* 15.32) drew attention to the high numbers of high-status women who appeared in the arena during Nero's reign. While acknowledging the lavish nature of the display, Tacitus was unequivocal about the disgrace of their crimes against class and gender. Not only were *gladiatrices*, no matter what their status, acting against Roman norms of female behaviour, but they were also somehow aping the laudable physical courage and male qualities (*virtus*) displayed by male gladiators. A particularly famous marble sculptural relief from Halicarnassus (modern Bodrum, Turkey, and now in the British Museum), depicts two female gladiators, neither apparently wearing a helmet; there is a helmet shown on either side of the accompanying inscription, which identifies them as Amazonia and Achillia. They both carry swords and rectangular shields, and wear the arm and leg defences similar to those worn by male gladiators. According to the inscription they were both granted a reprieve, presumably as a result of their good performance. According to Dio (76.16), in AD 200 Septimius Severus forbade women to fight in single combat.

Although the evidence for women fighting in the arena presents difficulties, it is quite clear that some women (and high-status women drew particular comment) much admired men who fought in the arena, at least for their manly courage, virility and physical attributes. Juvenal (*Satires* 6.110 -15) recounted the story of Eppia, a noblewoman, who had amorous feelings for a gladiator and eloped with him to Egypt even though he was battered and scarred from many fights; as Juvenal says, it can all be explained by the fact that he is a gladiator. A modern parallel can be found in the attraction and manageability of Sumo wrestlers.

The amphitheatre
Gladiatorial displays are first and foremost associated with the amphitheatre, but as a permanent building type it was a development of the late Republic. In Republican Rome, gladiatorial displays were staged in the political and symbolic heart of the city, the Forum Romanum. It has been suggested that the ovoid plan of early permanent amphitheatres was

modelled on the shape of the wooden seating that was erected for specta-tors of these displays around this piazza. Under the paving of the Forum was found a central corridor with four lateral arms bisecting it at regular distances 15 metres apart. The alignment of the central corridor is parallel with the Basilica Iulia, which was inaugurated in 46 BC, suggesting that the galleries may have been installed at about the same time. They gave access into the Forum through twelve shaft openings. Traces of installa-tions in these galleries are reminiscent of the system of cages and pulleys that would later be installed beneath some developed amphitheatres of the imperial period for winching performers and animals up into the arena. To improve facilities for the spectators further, Julius Caesar apparently stretched awnings over the whole forum on several occasions (Pliny, *Natural History* 19.23).

As an explanation for the permanent amphitheatre's elliptical form, Pliny the Elder (*Natural History* 36.116-20) offered the extraordinary building put up by C. Scribonius Curio in 52 BC for the funeral games in honour of his father. Scribonius 'built close to each other two very large wooden theatres, each poised and balanced on a revolving pivot. During the forenoon, a performance of a play was given in both of them and they faced in opposite directions so that the two casts should not drown out each other's words. Then, at a certain point the theatres were revolved (and it is agreed that after the first few days this was done with some of the spectators actually remaining in their seats), their corners met, and thus Curio provided an amphitheatre in which he produced fights between gladiators.'

There are a number of permanent late Republican period amphitheatres in Italy, but the only one which can be securely dated was constructed at Pompeii and dedicated between 70 and 65 BC (*CIL* X.852). C. Quinctius Valgus and Marcus Porcius, *duoviri* of the new colony established at Pompeii in 80 BC, paid for the structure with their own money in accord-ance with their magistracies. Interestingly, the building is referred to as '*spectacula*' in the inscription. The permanent amphitheatre is an archi-tectural form exclusively associated with the Romans, recognisable by its elliptical plan and arena, which is completely surrounded by seating. This is the literal meaning of the Greek word *amphitheatron*, which, from the time of Augustus, gradually came to be applied to this type of building. The amphitheatre at Pompeii was built on the eastern side of the city just within the town wall, and measures approximately 135 x 105 metres. It does not have the complicated system of vaulted substructures charac-teristic of many later amphitheatres, and the support for the seating was formed by upcast from digging the arena. At the upper level ran a retaining

wall strengthened by external buttresses and incorporating external staircases. A famous wall painting found in the peristyle garden of the House
of Actius Anicetus at Pompeii provides a unique contemporary view of
this building. The occasion is a riot which took place between rival fans
in AD 59, one of the earliest ancient examples of spectator violence in a
sporting context. The concession stands outside the amphitheatre are very
clear, but most importantly the fresco supplies the clearest depiction of the
awnings (*vela*, *velaria*) which provided shelter to the audience, the same
awnings which are often mentioned in advertisements in Pompeii for gladiatorial games. A number of amphitheatres, and theatres, have external corbels
for seating the masts which held the ropes for such awnings, but the exact
practicalities of how these functioned are still not understood.

The many of the earliest amphitheatres in Italy were provided in towns that
had particularly close ties with Rome, notably *coloniae* founded for army
veterans, for example Capua and Paestum. Such centres also provided the
context for the earliest amphitheatres in the provinces, for example at
Carmona in Spain, Corinth and Antioch-on-the-Orontes.

In Rome the first permanent amphitheatre was that of T. Statilius
Taurus, dedicated as late as 30 or 29 BC by one of Augustus' generals in
the southern Campus Martius, and financed by *manubiae* awarded to him
from the triumph he celebrated in 34 BC for securing the province of Africa
for Octavian (Dio 51.23.1). Little is known about it except that it was small
and built of stone and wood; Dio referred to it as a hunting theatre
(*theatron kunêgetikon*) and probably it was never used as a fully public
venue. It was destroyed in the great fire in AD 64. Several temporary
amphitheatres were built in the city: Julius Caesar's in the Forum Romanum,
and a particularly sumptuous one by Nero in AD 57 where it is claimed he
even held aquatic displays (Suetonius, *Nero* 12; Tacitus, *Annals* 13.31).

The most famous, and most inspirational, of all amphitheatres in the
Roman world is the Flavian Amphitheatre, better known today as the
Colosseum in Rome. This was begun by Vespasian in AD 75 on the site
of the drained lake of Nero's Domus Aurea. Though not fully completed,
it was dedicated in AD 80 by Titus after his father's death. Predictably, it
is the largest of all Roman amphitheatres with outer dimensions of 188 x
156 metres; the arena measures 80 x 54 metres. It had an estimated seating
capacity of 45-55,000. The concrete foundations were 12 metres deep,
supporting the 80 main load-bearing travertine piers on which rested the
façade, which itself rose to a height of nearly 50 metres. At each level of
the façade the arches were framed by engaged columns as in the Theatre
of Marcellus, the bottom storey being of the Doric order, the second Ionic
and the third Corinthian. The fourth storey, possibly not completed until

11. Amphitheatre, Nimes (France).

the reign of Domitian, was a plain wall with windows alternating with
Corinthian pilasters. Around the top of this level were two rows of corbels,
the mast supports for the ropes for the *velaria*. Beneath the now lost
wooden floor of the arena is an elaborate system of subterranean passages
and chambers where animals and gladiators were kept in readiness and
winched up to the arena level or let up along ramps. Such substructures
and their access points can be better appreciated in the amphitheatres at
Capua and Pozzuoli in Campania. Here the arena floors of concrete (*opus
caementicium*) are still in place and the trap doors for hauling up animal
cages can still be clearly seen.

To judge from the number of amphitheatres surviving in Italy, North
Africa, the Danube area and the western provinces, as well as much
epigraphic and sculptural evidence, gladiatorial displays were extremely
popular in those areas. Amphitheatres occur in large numbers, although
with much variation in size and design, for example in Italy, Verona, Alba
Fucens and Syracuse; in Spain, France and Germany, Mérida (Fig. 21),
Nimes (Fig. 11), Lyon and Trier; and in North Africa, Carthage, Lepcis
Magna and El Djem. Amphitheatres were also built in certain locations in
Britain, for example Silchester and Cirencester. Such structures were also
often found associated with legionary bases and other military installations.

Gladiators in the eastern provinces
By comparison, there are far fewer purpose-built amphitheatres known in
the eastern empire (Figs 12 and 13). Consequently, an outdated view held
that gladiatorial displays and their necessary venues were rare in the

12. Amphitheatre, Pergamum (Turkey).

13. Amphitheatre, Ptolemais (Libya).

eastern provinces. The view that the Greek provinces of the Roman empire were somehow more 'civilised' than Italy and the western provinces, and therefore could not have indulged in such blood sports has been a popular one, particularly among academics, since the nineteenth century. However, there is an undeniable wealth of evidence from the eastern provinces for gladiatorial and other arena displays, in the form of literary notices, epigraphy and iconography, as well as now the excavated remains of the gladiators themselves. Indeed, a large body of the sculptural and epigraphic material, particularly rich for Greece and Asia Minor, has been available since its publication by Louis Robert in the 1940s.

The earliest recorded instance of gladiatorial displays in the eastern Mediterranean was in a Hellenistic royal context when the Seleucid king Antiochus IV Epiphanes staged games at Daphne near Antioch in 166 BC (Polybius 30.25-6; Livy 41.20.10-13). It is clear from the accounts that such combats were unusual at this time; Polybius opined that Antiochus was aiming to emulate Aemilius Paulus, the victorious Roman general at the Battle of Pydna in north-east Greece just a few years before. The shows, which included both gladiatorial and animal displays, lasted thirty days and were equal in lavish scale to contemporary displays in Rome, though, according to Livy, at first these displays caused more alarm than anything else among the local population. Significantly, the gladiators were imported from Rome.

Twenty-two purpose-built amphitheatres have so far been identified in the East (this includes a number in the Danubian region, for example Diocletianopolis, Marcianopolis and Serdica). The earliest example was constructed at Antioch-on-the-Orontes, according to literary sources by Julius Caesar (Malalas 216.21-217.4; Libanius, *Orations* 2.219). Malalas refers to it as 'a place of single combat' (*monomachikon*). The simple form of this building, partly rock-cut, with no arena substructures, was probably similar to other contemporary amphitheatres known in Italy and the West, for example at Paestum and at Carmona. None of the amphitheatres in the Roman East have the monumentality of such structures in the West as at Nimes in the south of France, Mérida in Spain, or El Djem in Tunisia, except perhaps Pergamum (Fig. 12) or Cyzicus. Only Eleutheropolis in southern Israel has been properly excavated.

Not surprisingly, some of the earliest evidence, within a Roman context, for gladiatorial spectacles and animal displays in the eastern provinces is in connection with the cult of the deified emperors. An early first-century AD priest list of the cult of the Deified Augustus and Roma (*OGIS* 533) survives inscribed on one wall within the porch of the main cult temple in Ankara (Turkey). The form of some of the names of the priests indicates they are Galatians (e.g. Albiorix, Ateporix), of local descent, and their benefactions during their period of office are laid out in full. Gladiatorial games were the most prominent form of entertainment provided, though animal displays, including bull-fights, are also often mentioned. The presence of gladiatorial schools (*ludi*) and troupes (*familiae*) can probably also be associated with those cities in which provincial festivals were held, for example at Pergamum, Smyrna and Cyzicus in Turkey (*CIG* 3123; Galen VI.529; XIII.654; XIV.599-600). The *ludus* at

Pergamum was made famous by Galen, who was physician there for several years early in his career; later he became the court physician of Marcus Aurelius in the middle of the second century AD. There is also abundant epigraphic evidence from Aphrodisias for investment in gladiators. Tiberius Claudius Paulinus, high priest in the city during the first century AD, owned a troupe of gladiators (*monomachoi*) and condemned convicts (*katadikoi*). Another inscription mentions the gladiatorial *familia* of Zeno Hypsicles that comprised not only single combatants and convicts condemned to fight, but also bull-catchers (*taurokathaptai*).

In many of the cities of the East amphitheatres were never provided and other entertainment structures were adapted to accommodate gladiatorial and animal displays. As early as the first century AD gladiatorial contests were staged in theatres, for example in the Theatre of Dionysus in Athens. Many other theatres, as well as stadia, were adapted to a more multi-purpose function. This was achieved in a number of different ways. For example at Ephesus, the original iron railing around the orchestra was replaced by a wall 2 metres high formed by the removal of the lowest seats. On the other hand, some venues were built to be multi-purpose right from the start, for example the Hadrianic theatre at Stobi in Macedonia and the later first century AD stadium at Aphrodisias in Turkey, to accommodate a whole range of different types of entertainment.

Chapter 4

Animals and Spectacle

The use of animals for display, whether through personal or state patronage, had enjoyed a long history before the Romans recognised the benefits. For Egyptian pharaohs and Assyrian kings, hunting and the collecting of wild animals was a major pursuit, and allowed them to demonstrate their power and sovereignty over the natural world, a practice continued by the kings of Hellenistic Egypt. In 275-274 BC at Alexandria Ptolemy II Philadelphus included a great procession in the festivities associated with the religious festival, the Ptolemaieia, in honour of the deified Ptolemy I Soter. According to Athenaeus (*Deipnosophistae* v.201b-I), the animals were both wild and domesticated and included 130 Ethiopian sheep, 26 Indian oxen, 14 leopards, 16 panthers, an Ethiopian rhinoceros, and 24 huge lions. This bestial magnificence advertised the wealth of the Ptolemies and their influence in foreign lands; indeed some of the exotic animals may even have been bred in captivity.

This interest in amassing wild animals for private collections can be observed in later historical periods, for example the Royal Menagerie at the Tower of London, started in 1235 under Henry III, when, on the occasion of his marriage, he was presented with a wedding gift of three leopards by his cousin, the Holy Roman Emperor. From the end of the third century BC there was an increasingly popular fashion amongst Roman aristocrats to keep tame and wild animals, with some even taught to do tricks. Monkeys, particularly the barbary ape, were imported into Italy, and often appear in Roman art and literature as household pets or performing entertainments. The emperor Caracalla kept a number of tame lions which travelled with him, including one called Scimitar which ate and slept in his room (Dio 78.7.2-3). Elagabalus (*Historia Augusta, Elagabalus* 25.1) had tame maneless lions whose teeth and claws had been removed; the emperor delighted in turning them loose in guests' bedrooms at night for comedic effect!

By the late Republic it was common practice for a wealthy landowner to have an enclosure or park on his estate, well-stocked with wild animals such as boar, wild goats and deer, which according to Columella (9.1) served to provide magnificence and pleasure, as well as profit. Such an enclosure was often referred to in the ancient sources as a *vivarium*; it is also the term that came to be used for the place where animals for the public games were kept. A third-century AD inscription (*CIL* 6.130, AD 241) mentions a *custos vivari*, an official whose specific responsibility was apparently to oversee such an area. According to Procopius (*Gothic War* I.23.13-18) there was a large *vivarium* just outside the city walls by the Pincian Hill. Whether this was the area used to house the large collection of animals formed in Rome by Gordian III (238-244) for his Persian triumph is uncertain. It was Philip the Arab who actually exhibited the animals as part of his celebration in 248 of the Ludi Saeculares and the 1000th birthday of Rome. This menagerie is listed in the *Historia Augusta* (*Gordians* 33.1.2): 32 elephants, 10 elks, 10 tigers, 60 tame lions, 30 tame maneless lions, 10 hyenas, 6 hippopotamuses, a rhinoceros, 10 white or very large lions (the original text is unclear), 10 giraffes, 20 wild asses and 40 wild horses. An imperial elephant park at Laurentum to the south of Rome was under the control of a *procurator ad elephantos* (*CIL* 6.8583; *ILS* 1578), and was where an official stock of elephants was maintained. Elephants were actually bred in captivity there. Within Rome, the grounds of Nero's Golden House housed wild and domestic animals of all kinds (Suetonius, *Nero* 31).

The animal world was therefore an important one for the Romans to reference, exploit and display, and this is nowhere more evident than in the *venationes*, the animal hunts, of the Roman games. On one level Ptolemy's procession and the animal spectacles of the Roman world are similar in that they were a physical embodiment of the sense of burgeoning empire and expanding territorial control, coupled with control of the raw forces of nature. They differ, however, in terms of scale. Ptolemy Philadelphus' procession involved very small representative groups of the different animals, particularly the more exotic ones. For the Romans, the need to present variety and novelty on each occasion, in a form of inflationary competition between successive emperors, was all important. However, the most exotic and impressive animals continued to be major crowd-pleasers.

Early animal displays at Rome

The great animal shows of imperial Rome had a long prior history. The 'hunting' of animals such as hares, wild goats, wild boar and bulls in the Circus Maximus during festivals such as the Floralia was not unusual, but over time new contexts and new exotic *genera* were added. From the third century BC, animals were displayed in the city as living spoils of war – effectively living embodiments of Rome's acquisition of far-flung territories. Such overtly martial display is well-represented by the four Indian elephants exhibited in 275 BC in the triumph of Marcus Curius Dentatus after his victory over King Pyrrhus in Southern Italy (Pliny, *Natural History* 8.16). Elephants were highly symbolic animals given their role in eastern armies and their use as mounts by eastern potentates and by the Punic arch-enemy, and, of course, their colossal size was bound to impress. In 252 BC some 140 Carthaginian elephants were brought to Rome for the triumphal parade of Caecilius Metellus and then, according to Pliny (*Natural History* 8.16-17), they were hunted down in the Circus where they were killed with javelins, not so much as a demonstration of imperial power but more because the Romans were at a loss as to what to do with them subsequently. At this time elephants were also used as agents of public execution carrying out the imperial will; for example in 167 BC Aemilius Paulus executed foreign deserters from his army by having them crushed by elephants in Carthaginian style (Plutarch, *Aemilius Paulus* 16-23), and again in 146 BC similar action was taken by Scipio Aemilianus using elephants from North Africa (Valerius Maximus 2.7.13-14).

Over time increasing numbers of foreign animals were included in these displays, although details are obscure; the ostrich had certainly been seen in the Circus Maximus by the beginning of the second century BC (Plautus, *Persa* 199). The earliest recorded instance of a proper hunt (*venatio*) involving exotic animals took place in 186 BC as part of the victory games of Marcus Fulvius Nobilior (Livy 39.22.2). Exhibition of animals was part of the entertainment between races in the Circus Maximus; from this period onwards, the circus became the favoured location for such displays (Fig. 14). These Fulvian games were also important because they provided the context for the first appearance of Greek athletics in Rome, something that was subsequently to find only sporadic favour in the capital. The *venatio* involved lions and leopards, possibly from the East rather than from North Africa. In 169 BC (Livy 44.18.8) a show was given by the *aediles*, again in the Circus Maximus, which involved 63 *Africanae* (the usual term employed to indicate lions and/or leopards, irrespective of their geographical origin), 40 bears, and a number of elephants. Despite legislation in the second century BC which forbade the importation of animals from Africa into Italy (Pliny, *Natural History* 8.24), the tide could not be turned.

The atmosphere of intense political corruption of the first century BC stimulated the staging of animal displays with increasing frequency and elaboration, more often being held outside the traditional context of circus games. This set in motion an inflationary spiral as each individual *trium-*

14. 'Campana plaque' depicting *venationes* in the circus.

phator aimed to outdo his rivals in terms of the range and numbers of animals involved in his spectacles.

Thus by the imperial period animal displays were a firm favourite in Roman spectacle, but they could vary considerably in terms of scale, context and nature. In modern scholarship the term *venatio* (plural *venationes*) is used to refer to the full range of animal displays:

- presentations of exotic animals;
- shows with trained animals performing tricks;
- hunting displays with hunters on horseback and on foot, often with hunting dogs;
- fights between professional *venatores* (beast fighters) and dangerous wild beasts;
- fights between different types of wild animals;
- executions of criminals condemned to die as *damnati ad bestias*.

The animals

As we have seen, the earliest animals displayed in Rome were the elephants from the campaigns against Pyrrhus in the first half of the third century BC; these were almost certainly Indian elephants, but from the literary and artistic sources it is clear that it was North Africa which supplied a large proportion of the elephants and other wild animals for the Roman games. As Rome's influence in the region increased, so did the

Romans' capacity to stage *venationes* in more elaborate ways, using not only the animals but often also the hunters from their original regions as well. In 94 BC Sulla pitted lions against native spearmen expressly acquired for the purpose from King Bocchus of Mauretania (Seneca, *De Brevitate Vitae* 13.5); the king may also have supplied the lions. In 61 BC the curule *aedile* L. Domitius Ahenobarbus matched 100 Numidian bears against the same number of Ethiopian hunters (Pliny, *Natural History* 8.54). Such displays were therefore injected with a great deal of reality, as well as demonstrating an individual patron's influence in far-flung regions. Many of these animals can no longer be found north of the Sahara, and it has been traditional to suggest that the Romans effectively hunted them to regional extinction in their quest to supply animals for the arena in ever-increasing numbers and variety. However, there is still much debate about this among modern scholars. Nevertheless, Africa did supply beasts in huge quantities; the abundant and exotic fauna as well as the area's proximity to Italy and the role that region played in Rome's history in the last few centuries of the Republic gave it enormous symbolic importance.

The animals most often referred to in the sources and which are most frequently depicted in artworks are elephants, big cats and bears. This probably reflects their popularity and visual potency rather than necessarily their frequency of appearance in the arena. It is important to remember that the literary evidence takes particular notice of the extraordinary occasions, for example, the first *genus* appearance, the largest number to date of a certain animal, and the greatest variety of *genera* present.

Elephants. The elephant most often found in Roman spectacle is probably equivalent to the modern African Forest elephant (*Loxodonta cyclotis*), which is smaller than the Bush elephant (*Loxodonta Africana*). That elephants were common in the North African littoral is indicated by the artistic evidence; for example, a mosaic from El Djem shows the goddess Africa sporting an elephant headdress, emphasising a close association at least in Roman perception. The first recorded elephant fights in Rome, as opposed to elephants being used as part of a triumphal display, took place in 99 BC when C. Claudius Pulcher was *aedile*; twenty years later the first fight between an elephant and bulls took place (Pliny, *Natural History* 8.7). They could also be taught tricks, and Pliny referred to mind-boggling acts such as tightrope-walking and dancing elephants (Pliny, *Natural History* 8.2); it is in such benign performances, with some exceptions, that they most often appeared in public spectacle in Rome from the Augustan period onwards. Although Pliny also cited elephants performing duels resembling gladiatorial fights, elephants were rarely killed as part of a spectacle. They were held in a certain amount of affection, being considered to display moral steadfastness and loyalty; this is almost certainly why during a huge set of games held by Pompey in 55 BC, on the last day when 20 elephants were pitted against Gaetulian javelin-throwers, the crowd came to pity the elephants as one by one they were killed (Pliny, *Natural History* 8.7; Cicero, *Ad Familiares* 7.1.3). On the odd occasion after this that they did appear in the arena pitched against other animals, for example in Titus' games celebrating the dedication of the Colosseum in AD 80, the usual foe was a bull (Martial, *On Spectacles* 22); such a pairing, with the elephant carrying a mahout, is depicted on a mosaic found on the Aventine in Rome.

Big cats. In the ancient sources, the term '*Africanae*' came to be used collectively for lions, leopards and other big cats, irrespective of their origin. From the first century BC these big cats appeared in huge numbers in the arena. The Romans acquired most of their lions from Libya (they are a common motif in mosaics from North Africa); certainly the largest specimens came from there, but lions also could be found in Syria and Mesopotamia. They first appeared in Roman spectacle in the early second century BC (Pliny, *Natural History* 8.20); Sulla staged a combat involving 100 lions in 93 BC, but there are actually far fewer instances of lions in the games in Rome in the imperial period, particularly after Nero's reign. This may have had something to do with increasing cost; by the early fourth century AD the maximum price for a top quality lion for the arena is listed in the Diocletian's *Edict of Maximum Prices* as 600,000 sesterces (possibly somewhere in the region of £4 million today), and a second-class lion as 400,000 sesterces (about £2.5 million).

Leopards appeared in much larger numbers, also being found in both North Africa and Syria. They first appeared in Rome in the games of Marcus Aemilius Scaurus (58 BC) when 150 were shown. Leopards are often depicted in mosaics, and a particularly gruesome example can be seen on the Villa Borghese mosaic. This depicts a number of leopards, all dead or in the process of dying very painfully with blood pouring from wounds caused by spears. Only slightly less gruesome are the scenes painted on the lower parts of the vaults covering the *frigidarium* of the Hunting Baths at Lepcis Magna; on one side of the room these show a leopard hunt. Six leopards, three of whose names survive – RAPIDVS, FVLGENTIVS, GABATIVS(?) – are hunted by *venatores*, four of whose names can be made out – NVBER, [V?]ICENTIVS, [L?]IBENTIVS, BICTOR. Blood flows freely from the wounds inflicted by the hunters' spears. On the opposite wall is a lion hunt. These detailed paintings have suggested to many scholars that these baths belonged to a guild (*colle-*

gium) of either professional fighters or merchants who dealt in animals for the arena. Such an association, the Telegenii, is well-attested in inscriptions across central North Africa from Timgad in eastern Algeria to the towns of eastern Tunisia, and is the subject of a famous mosaic now in the Sousse Museum (Fig. 15).

Of all the big cats the tiger was extremely rare and on most occasions was exhibited for its novelty effect. In 11 BC Augustus was the first to exhibit a tame tiger, and tigers formed part of the display in the celebrations of Domitian's Sarmatian Wars in AD 93 (Martial, *Epigrams* 8.26). In the early third century, in games held to celebrate the marriage of Elagabalus, 51 tigers were apparently killed (Dio 79.9.2), the largest number of which there is a definite record.

Bears. Bears are not today associated with North Africa, but literary and iconographic sources indicate that Africa supplied a large quantity for the arena; both Libyan and Numidian bears are mentioned, but they also came from Greece, Asia Minor and northern Europe, as well as Italy itself. The numbers of bears recorded in the arena are larger than for any other animal and they are the only species where hunting for the spectacles may have had an effect on the size of the population: 400 bears under Caligula (AD 37), 300 bears under Claudius (AD 41) and another 400 under Nero (Dio 59.7.3; 60.7.3; 61.9.1). Bears might be pitched against human combatants or against other animals, for example on the Zliten mosaic a bear is shown fighting a bull, the animals chained together to ensure they cannot ignore each other (Fig. 28). Bears appear in a number of other North African mosaics, often named. Intriguingly, there are two possible references to polar bears in the sources. Martial, in his description of the Colosseum inauguration (AD 80) (*On Spectacles* 15.3.4), referred to a bear which 'had been king of all the beasts beneath the Arctic sky'. This could have merely meant a bear from northern Germany or Caledonia. However, Calpurnius Siculus (*Eclogues* 65.66), in the context of Nero's great games (AD 57), described bears that chased seals, the chief prey of polar bears. Again it is perfectly possible that what was meant were bears from northern Europe that had been taught to swim.

Bulls. Bulls were frequently displayed in the arena and were often pitted against bears or elephants. The first recorded fight between bears and bulls took place in 79 BC (Pliny, *Natural History* 8.7), and Seneca witnessed a fight between bulls and bears tied together (*De Ira* 3.43.2). Bull-fighting was also popular and is attested at Pompeii (*ILS* 5053). Julius Caesar was credited with the introduction of Thessalian bull fighting in his games of 46 BC (Suetonius, *Julius* 29); this seems to have been an ancient form of rodeo in which bulls were pursued on horseback and then wrestled to the ground. A second-century AD relief from Asia Minor (Ashmolean Museum, Oxford) appears to depict something like this.

Rhinoceroses. It was Pompey who exhibited the first rhinoceros in his great games of 55 BC (Pliny, *Natural History* 8.29). The sources are in disagreement about the exact nature of this particular animal – whether it was a two-horned African variety, possibly from Ethiopia, or a single-horned Indian rhinoceros. The single-horned was more commonly exhibited in Rome, and is depicted on the Great Hunt Mosaic at Piazza Armerina. The African variety occurred in Titus' games in AD 80. At first its keepers could not get it to fight, but when they did evoke a response it killed a bear by tossing it in the air (Martial, *On Spectacles* 22). Rhinoceroses were always unusual, but *venationes* involving a number of them are known under Antoninus Pius and Commodus (*Historia Augusta, Antoninus Pius* 10.9; Dio 73.10.3), but their variety is not known.

Hippopotamuses. To the Greek and Roman worlds, the hippopotamus was essentially a denizen of the Nile; it was depicted on the first-century BC Palestrina mosaic depicting the Nile in flood. The first hippopotamus to be seen in Rome was in the games of Aemilius Scaurus in 58 BC when he was *aedile*, but their involvement in Roman spectacles was more for their novelty and display value than their combativeness. However, Commodus is recorded to have killed five with his own hand (Dio 73.10).

Crocodiles. The games of Aemilius Scaurus saw another animalistic first in the display of five crocodiles in a temporary tank (Pliny, *Natural History* 8.40). Of all the Nilotic animals, nothing fascinated the Romans more than the crocodile; Pliny (*Natural History* 8.37) called it 'a curse on four legs'. Although it was always associated with Egypt, it also came from East Africa. Augustus, during the games to celebrate the dedication of the Temple of Mars Ultor (2 BC), exhibited 36 crocodiles in a custom-dug basin in the Circus Flaminius (Dio 60.10.8). This spectacle ended with them being hunted to their deaths, a display of imperialism and autocracy, of the emperor taking into control that which was unusual, spectacular, naturally ferocious, and Egyptian. These may have been the same crocodiles mentioned by Strabo (17.1.44) which were accompanied by men from Tentyra in the Nile valley who prepared a pool with a platform on one side. These men would enter the pool and drag the crocodiles up onto the platform in nets so that they could be seen by the spectators, then drag them back into the water.

Ostriches. The ostrich appeared in Roman spectacles in some numbers. It was certainly to be seen in Rome by the early second century BC; Plautus (*The Persian* 199) comments on its speed. It is clear from North African mosaics that they were hunted in that region. Their popularity in the arena was guaranteed not only because of their comedic run but also by their aggressive and vicious tendencies. According to Herodian (1.15.3-6), on one occasion Commodus shot the heads off a number of ostriches with crescent-shaped arrowheads. He apparently held up the heads to watching senators as if to say that this was what would happen to them – all the while the decapitated bodies were still doing 'headless chicken' impressions. Gordian I, along with a wide range of wild animals, kept 300 red Moorish ostriches which were eventually killed in games (*Historia Augusta, Gordians* 3).

Giraffes. The giraffe did not make many appearances in the Roman arena. It first appeared in the great games of 46 BC under Julius Caesar, when it was described as a cross between a leopard and a camel (*camelop-ardalis*: Pliny, *Natural History* 8.27; Dio 53.23.1); Pliny notes that it was admired for its looks rather than any ferocity. The only instance of a giraffe being killed for the spectators' delight is when Commodus killed a giraffe with his own hand (Dio 73.11).

A modern perception has it that there was little variety in these animal displays, but in fact it was enormous. The aim, as with gladiatorial combat, was to have a balanced and fair fight, but also one which was interesting, one where the true nature of the animals involved could be appreciated by the spectators. Different pairings appear in iconography and literature, ranging from the more 'regular' ones such as bull against elephant or bear, to the rather more unlikely pairing of a lion against a crocodile.

After the middle of the first century AD, Africa and the East still provided animals for the emperors' displays in Rome, but in smaller numbers; lions and leopards are rarely recorded in large numbers after the time of Nero, although this might be a product of the source material rather than reflecting actual practice. However, in AD 281 the emperor Probus was still able to display 400 big cats in the amphitheatre, and in the Circus, specially transformed into a forest, he staged a great hunt involving a wide range of animals including ostriches, boars, stags and gazelles during his triumphal celebrations.

Even in the third century there was still scope to impress the Roman population with exotic animals. In the reign of Septimius Severus 'Horses of the Sun, which resemble tigers', were carried off from an island in the Red Sea (Dio 75.14.3; 77 6.2); this was the *hippotigris* (literally the tiger-horse), the zebra, which probably became imperial property, only for some of them at least to be killed in a show early on in Caracalla's reign.

To judge from the Italian epigraphic evidence, similar shows occurred throughout the peninsula into the third century AD. African beasts (*bestiae Africani* and *ferae Libycae*) are mentioned for example at Allifae, Telesia and Samnium (*ILS* 5059-61), as well as bears and herbivores. Where numbers are given, which is unusual, they are small. In the provinces, the scale and variety must have been at a reduced level, possibly more reliant on locally available animals as a result.

Capture and transport of animals

In the Republic, the hunting and capture of animals for shows seems to have been more impromptu, with little or no organisation or infrastructure. Animals were supplied for prominent magistrates by their 'contacts' in the provinces as required. However, by the imperial period the demand had become so great that in order to keep a supply of animals for Rome's arenas a sophisticated and complex organisation was required, with a huge investment in time, money and manpower. Because many of these animals were difficult to maintain in good condition, they were very much an illustration of conspicuous consumption, also providing a direct expression of Rome's imperial ambition and world-wide power, and at a more personal level, an individual's wealth, status and power.

By the first century AD the Roman army was involved in this supply process. Evidence from across the empire attests to the fact that the capturing and transport of exotic animals was an important part of a soldier's duty. A late first/early second century AD letter surviving from Egypt written by one Antonius Proculus, an auxiliary soldier stationed in the Eastern Desert of Egypt, described hunting for a variety of animals for a whole year. Another document from Egypt, the early third-century AD *Cestes* of Julianus Africanus, recommends the capture of wild animals as a type of military exercise and gives detailed instructions for the apprehending of wild lions. A number of inscriptions from Rome and the Danube region mention *venatores immunes* who seem to have been soldiers exempted from certain routine duties in return for involvement in animal-capturing expeditions.

The mosaics of North Africa provide one major source for the logistics and practice of capturing animals for the arena. The hunt mosaic from the Maison d'Isguntus at Hippo Regius (Algeria) illustrates a hunt for and capture of a lion, a lioness and three leopards who have been driven into a semicircular area defined by nets and the shields of armed men, where a cage awaits them. Behind the latter is a group of unsuspecting cows and sheep serving as a lure. The Great Hunt Mosaic of Piazza Armerina illustrates not only the hunting and capture of animals, but also their loading onto ships. An elephant is led on a chain up a gangway; an ostrich is rather incongruously carried onboard in the arms of a very calm-looking man (Fig. 15); a tiger and a rhinoceros require a number of men to control

15. Great Hunt Mosaic, Piazza Armerina (Sicily). Detail of ostrich.

them. The mosaic also emphasises that it was not just exotic animals that were hunted and captured in great numbers; various varieties of deer and gazelle were also required for the larger hunting displays. These are shown being driven by horsemen into a netted enclosure. Soldiers are involved throughout the process.

A number of 'animal-catalogue' mosaics also survive. These depict animals exhibited in a *munus*, with a single representative standing for the overall number of each type indicated in an accompanying inscription; a particularly good example is in a house near the amphitheatre at Carthage

(Tunisia). Three pairs of leopards are shown fighting each other, but other animals are shown singly and not in combat – a boar, an ostrich, a bear, a bull, some deer and antelopes. Under the bear the inscription NXL (40) appears, under the ostrich NXXV (25). In another mosaic from Radès (Tunisia), animals are again shown with a number, but the bears are also individually named, presumably members of a troupe especially trained to perform tricks. Presumably such trained animals would seldom have been killed in the arena.

The sailing season in the Mediterranean limited the effective transport period to between March or April and October. Pliny the Younger wrote to his friend Maximus in commiseration that his games at Verona had been spoilt because big cats which he had ordered had been delayed by the weather (*Letters* 6.34). In particular the scale of some of the spectacles in the capital involved huge co-ordination efforts; in his *Res Gestae* (22) Augustus claimed that in 26 *venationes* some 3,500 animals were killed. In the games for the inauguration of the Colosseum (AD 80), 9,000 animals were killed over 100 days (Suetonius, *Titus* 7.3). According to Dio, in games held in AD 107 after Trajan's return from Rome having defeated Dacia, 11,000 were killed over 123 days (Dio 68.15). These animals had to be fit for display and be able to perform well. They had to be fed and watered during transport and then kept, presumably for as short a time as possible, to preserve their ferocity, ready for their star turn in the arena. Symmachus, consul in AD 391, lamented in a letter of AD 401 that crocodiles brought in for a spectacle had effectively been on hunger strike for 50 days (*Epistles* 6. 43). Crocodiles were particularly difficult to transport, not least because of their cold-blooded nature requiring careful regulation of their body temperature. Equally they will not eat if they are boxed in; effectively they become depressed, something of which Symmachus had rather painful first-hand experience!

To emphasise the logistical challenge of moving these animals, it is worth examining a nineteenth-century example. No hippopotamus had been seen in Europe after the Roman period until 1850 when one was brought to the London Zoological Gardens. This was a present given by the Pasha of Egypt as a result of extreme persuasive pressure by the British Consul. A whole army division was occupied in capturing it, then it took five to six months to reach Cairo. From Alexandria it travelled in a specially constructed steamer with a large freshwater tank of 400 gallons capacity which had to be renewed on a daily basis. Two cows and ten goats barely satisfied its milk requirements; it would have required a daily food intake of 150 lb. This was just one animal, whereas thousands were required for some of the Roman spectacles.

The *venatores* and *bestiarii*

Originally the *venatores* were professional hunters and animal handlers. The *bestiarius*, later equated with the *venator*, was at first armed with a spear and condemned to fight the beasts with a high probability of death. Over time the *venatores*, and some of the *bestiarii*, were trained and, like the gladiators, even though they were *infames*, could become famous. Carpophoros, who appeared in Titus' games in AD 80, was much praised for his many kills (Martial, *On Spectacles* 15.22, 27). *Venatores* appeared in a number of guises. They hunted relatively harmless game, such as deer, ostriches and wild asses, using spears on horseback or on foot; essentially these displays were a demonstration of equestrian and weapons skills.

A number of artistic representations give some idea of how they were equipped. One of the so-called 'Campana' terracotta reliefs shows *venatores* wearing helmets, loincloths and greaves, and carrying swords, looking not unlike contemporary gladiators, but this might have been unusual (Fig. 14). Certainly after the mid-first century AD, *venatores* were shown dressed more like ordinary hunters, with only a *tunica* and short or knee-length wrappings on their legs (*fasciae crurales*), and armed with a hunting spear (*venabulum*), for example on a funerary relief from Pompeii (now in the Naples Museum); one is fighting a bull with his spear, the other is in combat with a boar. Three other fighters have been thrown to the ground by an attacking bear. The *venatores* on the Zliten mosaic are similarly clothed. A second century mosaic from the Roman villa at Nennig in Germany figures *venatores* wearing what appear to be knee-breeches and very broad belts plus leg wrappings; some of the fighters have small decorated breastplates.

The third-century AD Magerius mosaic from a villa at Smirat near Sousse (Tunisia) gives the most comprehensive account of animal displays (Fig. 16). It commemorates a *ludus* funded by the eponymous local worthy. It depicts four named members of the troupe of animal-fighters along with four leopards, also named, all of which are severely wounded. At the centre of the mosaic is a figure of a herald holding a tray with four bags on it. On either side is a lengthy inscription, in which the display is referred to as a '*munus*'; the troupe is identified as the Telegenii and an appeal is made to the audience for support for the sum of 500 *denarii* for each leopard from the would-be *munerarius*, Magerius. To the right of the herald is the *acclamatio*, the audience's enthusiastic response to the requested payment; on each of the four bags is a symbol denoting 1000, indicating that Magerius responded by paying 1000 *denarii* for each animal, double the going rate. Other evidence from North Africa suggests that this action was not that unusual. Also depicted on the mosaic is a figure of Diana, goddess of hunting, who

16. Magerius Mosaic, Smirat (Tunisa).

approaches from the left carrying millet stalks which were probably the emblem of the Telegenii, and Bacchus who carries a type of spear topped with a crescent, apparently another feature peculiar to depictions of this troupe. Yet another figure, which appears twice, has been identified as Magerius himself. This mosaic, either on the floor of the *triclinium* or a bath suite, represents a physical symbol of Magerius' power and wealth, keeping alive the *kudos* already accrued from the *munus* itself.

The Telegenii are the best known troupe of *venatores* in the North African evidence, and together such professional groups have been termed '*sodalitates venatorum*' by modern scholars. With their close knowledge of wild animals, such groups were probably also involved in the acquisition, transport and trade of animals for the spectacles.

In Rome animal fighters were trained in the Ludus Matutinus, its name derived from the fact that, in large games, animal fights traditionally took place in the morning (Seneca, *Letters* 7). This training school, possibly founded as early as the time of Caligula, was located close to the Colosseum and, just like the Ludus Magnus, was under direct imperial control (*CIL* 6.352).

Animal displays in the provinces
Animal displays were popular across the empire, but they were far from homogeneous, being much more dependent on locally available animals. As a result, spectacles involving exotic animals were far less frequent.

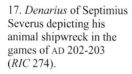

17. *Denarius* of Septimius
Severus depicting his
animal shipwreck in the
games of AD 202-203
(*RIC* 274).

There were exceptions to this, for example the *munus* of Magerius, but often the non-visual sources are very unspecific about the types of animals involved. For example, Hadrian gave a large scale *venatio* of 1000 beasts staged in the Panathenaic stadium in Athens (*Historia Augusta, Hadrian* 19); the animal displays listed in the Galatian priest list, with the exception of bulls, are equally vague.

The venue for animal displays also varied. In Rome, initially the Circus Maximus was the preferred location. Subsequently, other locations were used, for example the Amphitheatre of Statilius Taurus, called a 'hunting theatre' (*theatron kunêgetikon*) by Dio (51.23.1), and later the Colosseum, though the Circus remained the favoured location. A memorable occasion was in AD 202/3 when Septimius Severus, as part of his *decennalia* celebrations, dressed up an animal display as a great shipwreck. A huge mock ship was hauled into the Circus and when it broke apart 400 animals poured out, including lions, leopards, bears, ostriches and wild asses (Dio 76.1.3-5) (Fig. 17). In Italy and the provinces, where the variety of locations was much more limited, animal displays were also staged at a range of different locations. The amphitheatre was of course still used, as indicated by the scenes of animal hunts on the podium walls of the amphitheatres at Pompeii and Mérida. The small amphitheatre at Maktar (Tunisia) was specifically equipped for such displays. There are no arena substructures but entrances in the podium wall gave access for both human and animal combatants (Fig. 18). In the eastern provinces, the stadium, and some theatres were either provided with the necessary facilities from the beginning, such as the Hadrianic theatre at Stobi, or modified at some point so that animal displays could take place in them. The former is certainly the case in the later first-century stadium at Aphrodisias (Turkey) and the Panathenaic Stadium rebuilt in the mid-second century AD by Herodes Atticus in Athens, and the recently excavated Herodian period

18. Amphitheatre, Maktar (Tunisia). The doorways into the arena contained a smaller, and separate, access for animals from cages.

structure at Caesarea Maritima was similarly a multi-purpose entertainment venue from the outset.

Modifications, such as in the theatre at Philippi in Greece, involved the provision of nets supported on timber uprights which protected the spectators from inadvertent audience participation. Big cats can jump fences 4 metres high, so most venues required extra audience security on top of the podium wall, which was usually no more than 2 metres in height at best. No depiction of such an installation survives, though the cuttings in stonework can be discerned, for example in the Colosseum and the stadium at Aphrodisias. However, Calpurnius Siculus (*Eclogues* 7.50-6) describes an arrangement in Nero's temporary amphitheatre on the Campus Martius in Rome, built in AD 57, comprising a fence and netting topped by some kind of device with horizontally-mounted metal rollers which, by turning, would prevent an animal gaining purchase and thus being able to jump over. The rather comedic effect would no doubt have appealed to a Roman audience, while frustrating and angering the animals even further.

Chapter 5

Naumachiae and Aquatic Displays

Novelty and extravagance were the watchwords of public entertainment in Rome, and the aquatic displays of the capital in the late first century BC and first century AD supremely capture its spectacular essence. The *naumachia* or *stagnum* was an artificial basin constructed for large-scale aquatic displays, and the former term came to be used for the spectacles themselves, particularly sea-battle re-enactments. Such large-scale naval exhibitions had apparently been held by Scipio Africanus in the context of military display and training. In 40 BC Sextus Pompey staged a battle at sea off the coast at Rhegium in southern Italy for the entertainment of his troops, involving a fight to the death between prisoners of war (Dio 48.19). Nevertheless, such large-scale spectacles were unusual and became the preserve of the capital. There were also smaller-scale displays involving water ballets, not necessarily of a high cultural calibre.

Aquatic displays in Rome
The first recorded public *naumachia* was staged by Julius Caesar in a specially built basin in the Campus Martius in 46 BC (Suetonius, *Julius* 39.4). The basin was filled in after the event and nothing now survives to give any indication of size. However, to judge from the numbers of ships and men involved, it was a construction on a very large scale. The battle was between two fleets representing Tyre and Egypt, a characteristically plausible context although not based on an actual historical event. The fleets comprised a variety of ships, with two, three and four banks of oars manned by prisoners of war numbering some 6,000 (Dio 45.17).

In 2 BC, as part of the celebrations for the inauguration of the Temple of Mars Ultor in his new Forum, Augustus staged large-scale water displays. For these he built a huge artificial lake, referred to in the sources as a *stagnum* (Dio 55.10.7). This was located on the right bank of the Tiber, in the area of what is now Trastevere. The *Res Gestae* (23) provides colossal dimensions of 1800 x 1200 Roman feet (approximately 536 x 357 metres). These dimensions give a figure of somewhere in the region of 270,000 cubic metres of water which was provided by a new and largely

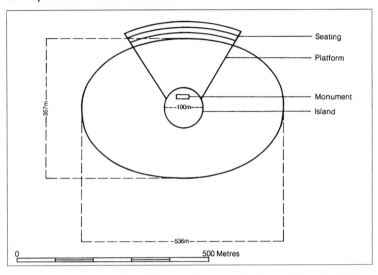

Seating

Platform

Monument

Island

---100m---

357m

---536m---

0   500 Metres

19. Suggested reconstruction of Augustus' *stagnum* in Rome (Rabun Taylor).

subterranean aqueduct, the *aqua Alsietina* (Frontinus, *Aqueducts* 11.22), drawn from a lake to the north-west of the city, Lake Martignano (the ancient Lake Alsietinus). The water inside must have been at least 1.7 metres deep to allow for the use of oars as well as realistic drowning! It is clear that the *stagnum* had an island but the overall shape is not certain. It may have been planned as an ellipse, giving maximum all-round visibility for the spectators, but close examination of the orientation of modern buildings in the area has suggested that it had a more rectangular shape (Figs 19 and 20). Ships were brought into the basin by a canal which connected to the Tiber. The Augustan display was a re-enactment of the Battle of Salamis and involved 30 ships, both biremes and triremes, all with battering rams, plus a number of smaller vessels. Three thousand soldiers and a commensurate number of oarsmen took part in the battle.

The basin continued in use certainly until the time of Titus, when it was used for some of the larger displays staged for the inauguration of the Colosseum in AD 80. According to Martial a number of mythological re-enactments involving water were accommodated in the Colosseum, for example Leander's midnight swim (actually probably an execution in the pretence of a re-enactment) and water ballets, effectively displays of synchronized swimming Roman style which might have included nudity and themes of love and sex. However, there were also larger-scale sea-battles; according to Suetonius these were held 'on the old *nauma-*

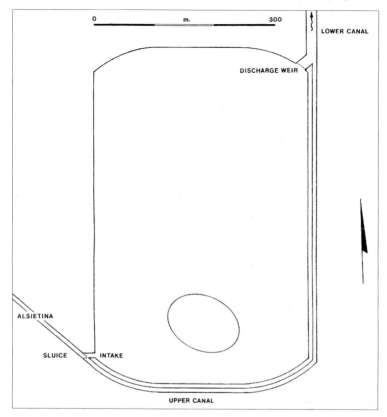

20. Reconstruction of Augustus' stagnum in Rome, according to Rabun Taylor.

chia' (Suetonius, *Titus* 7.3), that is Augustus' *stagnum*, and he made no mention of aquatic performance held within the Flavian amphitheatre.

Dio (46.25.2-4) also mentioned use of Augustus' *stagnum* for a naval battle between the Syracusans and the Athenians. This was a large-scale and complex spectacle which became a land battle when an assault was made on a structure on an island within the 'sea'. However, he also claimed that 'Titus filled the above mentioned theatre [he meant the Colosseum] suddenly with water … He introduced also men in boats who engaged in a sea-battle there, impersonating the Corcyreans and the Corinthians.' This has created heated debate among scholars about whether or not the Flavian amphitheatre really was capable of supporting large-scale water spectacles at the time of inauguration. Despite recent architectural and archaeological work on the substructures beneath the arena, there is still no consensus on the subject. This area of the building was much re-modelled by Domitian and later emperors. It is true that it is lined with waterproof mortar (*opus signinum*) and that there are drains which would allow the evacuation of water in some quantity, but there has been no identification of a large enough permanent water supply system to allow the arena to be flooded. Equally, there have been no adequate estimates of the amount of time it might have taken to both fill and empty the arena if it was flooded. The smaller displays referred to by Martial could have been accommodated by a temporary pool or basin involving far less water movement.

Titus' displays marked a high point for water spectacles in Rome. Domitian apparently staged a naval battle in the amphitheatre as well as sea-battles in a 'new location', according to Suetonius (*Domitian* 4). The biographer's account is so general and provides so few details that it is dangerous to make assumptions based on it. Trajan seems to have constructed a *naumachia* in the area to the north-west of Castel Sant'Angelo in the vicinity of the eighth-century church of the significantly named S. Pellegrino in Naumachia. Substantial masonry dated to the reign of Trajan survives indicating a rectangular structure that was smaller than Augustus' *stagnum*, but with a minimum capacity of 44,400 cubic metres. No specific water displays were recorded for Trajan's rule, but the structure may still have been functional to be used by Philip the Arab as part of the celebrations for the millennium of Rome in AD 247 (Aurelius Victor, *Caesars* 28).

On occasion, an area was created within an existing building for the purpose of aquatic display. Augustus displayed crocodiles in a temporary basin constructed in the Circus Flaminius and Caligula excavated and filled with water a basin in the Saepta Julia in order to display a single ship (Dio 59.10.5). Nero also staged several *naumachiae*. Although the sources are contradictory about the details and venues, it is clear that none of the latter were purpose-built. According to Suetonius (*Nero* 12) he staged a sea-battle on an artificial saltwater lake with sea monsters swimming in it. It may be the same event that is referred to by Dio (61.9.5), which involved flooding one of the theatres (which is unclear), with sea water and sea monsters and a battle between the Persians and the Athenians, presumably the Battle of Salamis. Nero then drained the structure and enacted land battles and other displays.

An extraordinary example of a natural setting for such displays took place in AD 52, when the emperor Claudius orchestrated a massive naval battle to commemorate the completion of a canal that would drain the Fucine Lake into the River Liris. This involved almost full-sized triremes and quariremes, with 19,000 combatants, most if not all of them criminals

(Tacitus, *Annals* 12.56). There were also rafts with various kinds of artillery operated by praetorians. The whole spectacle was watched by the emperor and his wife and the surrounding hillsides provided a natural seating area for the huge crowds of local inhabitants drawn to such an amazing sight. The battle was fought so realistically and with such courage that many of those forced to fight were freed.

Aquatic displays in the provinces

Such large and elaborate water displays were more a phenomenon of the capital and evidence from elsewhere in Italy and the provinces suggests they were far less common and on a much smaller scale. The amphitheatres at Verona and Mérida had shallow, almost cross-shaped basins (*fossae*) beneath the arena floors (Fig. 21); the shallow depth of these basins (approximately 1.25 m), and the presence of a water-supply, suggests that they may have been used for aquatic displays. The floorboards could presumably have been removed for an aquatic event and replaced for the rest of the programme. Naturally, any aquatic display performed in such a restricted basin would have been a very modest affair, with a few very small boats accommodated. Perhaps such structures were used for aquatic spectacles of a non-violent nature, such as some of those described by Martial during the inauguration of the Colosseum.

Aquatic spectacles may not have been very common in the provinces, but there is good archaeological evidence from late antiquity for a number of theatres, particularly in the eastern Mediterranean, being modified to

21. Amphitheatre, Mérida (Spain) 15-8 BC. View of arena with *fossa*.

allow the orchestra to be flooded. In the theatre at Paphos (Cyprus), in the later third century AD a wall was built at the base of the *cavea* seating around the orchestra so that it could be flooded. The theatre had already been modified with facilities for *venationes* and gladiatorial games. Similar modifications for water displays were carried out in other structures (see the next chapter).

Chapter 6

Spectacle in Late Antiquity

Compared to earlier periods, spectacle in late antiquity has received patchy attention, mainly due to the fragmentary nature of the evidence. The area best understood is chariot racing, which by the later fourth century had become highly politicised in both content and spectator involvement. Recent work at sites such as Aphrodisias has also greatly added to the picture. One of the biggest challenges is that presented by the role of Christianity in any changes which took place at this time. How was the range and type of public entertainments affected by new religious agendas? The traditional view holds that from the time of Constantine's rescript issued at Berytus in AD 325 gladiatorial games were banned, and that from the 390s Theodosius I authorised the destruction of 'pagan' buildings and the suppression of traditional public festivals and entertainments. Thus spectacles were transformed: no gladiators, very little theatre, no exotic and spectacular executions, nothing except chariot racing. This is a very simplistic view that does not take in the whole picture. There certainly was change, but the evolution of spectacle had as much to do with the social and economic environment as the religious. At least in some locations, the range of entertainments enjoyed was still very broad – and for a while it was still very bloodthirsty.

The form of spectacle in this period varied from one location to another, and a further problem is that the documentary evidence and archaeological evidence do not always align, indeed often they indicate rather different situations. It is not clear how far-reaching were the various pieces of legislation concerning public spectacle and performers. The growing body of Christian literature is very instructive about early Christian attitudes to public spectacle, but naturally it presented a very biased and imaginary view, in particular when concerned with 'persecution' of Christians and their appearance in the arena. Modern romantic ideas and the products of Hollywood have certainly helped to compound and prolong the biases.

Mid-fourth-century Rome enjoyed 175 festival days each year. The associated games comprised 10 days of gladiatorial *munera*, 64 of chariot racing (*circenses*) and 101 when dramatic *ludi* were staged. Thus, even at this late date, the full range of entertainments was still important, and presumably still popular, at least in the capital. Of course the inherent links with traditional cults and their celebration remained, as did the political significance of spectacles. Indeed, during the fifth and sixth centuries this latter element was greatly enhanced. From the time of Constantine, games, particularly and increasingly those held in the circus, were more closely linked to the emperor's actions, held to mark such events as his arrival at a major city, his victories in war and his anniversaries (of accession, etc). In addition the appointment of magistrates continued to be celebrated with games, certainly in Rome and Constantinople.

The anti-pagan edicts of Theodosius I at the very end of the fourth century which authorised the destruction of cult buildings and the suppression of public festivals and associated entertainments had a profound influence on urban life and probably accelerated changes in the forms of public entertainment. Yet a century later in AD 498, Anastasius issued an edict suppressing shows in all cities of the eastern empire. Nevertheless, *venationes* continued in Constantinople. Epigraphic evidence from Aphrodisias demonstrates that such spectacles continued there into the early sixth century AD. At the same time, athletic festivals were also still being held at Antioch and Apamea in Syria.

Spectacle and Christianity

Christian objections to Roman public spectacle were complex. There was already existing philosophical opposition to some of the performances, which was taken up by early Christians. At a fundamental level the circus and beast displays could continue provided that any pagan sacrifice and other explicitly pagan elements were removed from the procession and ceremonies. The philosophic tradition going as far back as the later first century AD had viewed gladiatorial displays as a particular threat to Greek culture, but it is interesting to note that there was little indication of objections on humanitarian grounds. For Christian writers, opposition was based on the grounds that the games were morally dangerous to the audience; the 'infamous' performers, it seems, were beyond hope! The objections were predictable but at their heart was the fear that Christians were habitually indulging in the behaviour which was being condemned. For St Augustine, bishop of Hippo at the end of the fourth century AD, the main concern was the psychological effect on the Christian soul of watching such entertainments, particularly gladiatorial displays. In his writings, the gladiator is characterised as evil and immoral, and the spectators as drunk on blood and violence. He recounts the story of Alypius who was taken to the amphitheatre in Rome by friends. He closed his eyes so he would not see the combat in the arena, but his curiosity got the better of him, and once he had seen the blood '… he drank in savageness at the same time. He did not turn away, but fixed his sight on it, and drank in madness without knowing it. He took delight in that evil struggle, and he became drunk on blood and pleasure. He was no longer the man entered there, but only one of the crowd that he had joined, and a true comrade of those who brought him there …' (Augustine, *Confessions* 6.8).

Similarly, for John Chrysostom, bishop of Constantinople at the end of the fourth and beginning of the fifth century AD, there was a spiritual danger and any damage was permanent for the spectator. In his *Contra ludos et theatra*, he likened the actress to a prostitute; as a result anyone who set foot in a theatre was not allowed to enter his church or share Christian communion. Traditional *infamia* writ large! Interestingly, Christian Roman and early Byzantine writers had no problems suppressing the pagan associations of chariot races and wild beast shows; and they are certainly not concerned with cruelty to animals. For some Christian writers, for example Tertullian (*c.* AD 160-240), the greatest concern was in relation to gladiatorial games because of the connection with funerals and hence the idea of renewal and resurrection, a potential usurpation of the salvatory symbolism of Christian religious sacraments.

The execution of criminals in the arena, an old and established Roman practice, was also unproblematic in late antiquity. This aspect of the judicial system continued and could be brutal. Indeed, from the time of Constantine there was an extended range of crimes which required torture and execution by fire or by wild beasts. For example, practitioners of magic and their accomplices faced death in the circus or the amphitheatre. The emperor Valentinian I in the later fourth century had the unpopular *praepositus* Rhodanus burned alive in the circus in Constantinople on charges of embezzlement.

An examination of the venues themselves can also be very instructive. Many were not torn down under Christian influence, and in some areas of public entertainment it actually took up to 200 years for terminal decline to set in. A number of buildings were modified for continued entertainment functions. Notably, a number of theatres in the eastern provinces were modified involving the cutting back of seating to create an arena-like area, for example at Ephesus, Cyrene in eastern modern Libya (Fig. 22), and the Theatre of Dionysos in Athens. These modifications varied in terms of date, with some possibly as early as the late first and second centuries AD, and are sometimes ambiguous as to the exact form of spectacle presented. Most of the modifications seem to have accommodated

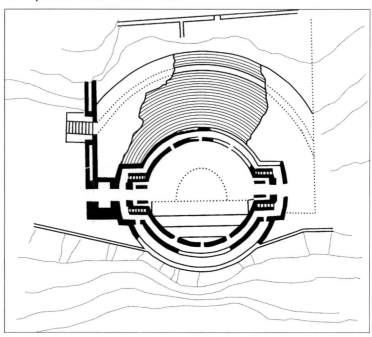

22. Theatre, Cyrene (Libya). Plan. Original Greek theatre converted into an amphitheatre in second/third century AD.

gladiatorial displays, where the podium wall was only 1.5-2 metres high, but supplementary nets could also have been rigged on top of these walls to create extra protection during *venationes*. The theatre at Aphrodisias was also modified for gladiatorial combats, but other types of entertainment, such as acrobatics, were also accommodated, as evidenced by a graffito on the stage building depicting a tight-rope walker.

Gladiatorial displays
The evidence for gladiatorial displays in late antiquity is contradictory and its interpretation is especially influenced by modern preconceptions. Constantine's rescript of AD 325 is usually interpreted as having banned gladiatorial games. It did forbid gladiators and ruled that criminals should be condemned to work in the mines (*ad metallas*) instead of fighting in the arena, but there was also perhaps an economic dimension to this. Previously Christians had often been condemned to the mines, but with tolerance of their cult there followed a shortage of such manpower. The contrariness of this legislation is highlighted by the fact that just ten years before (AD 315) Constantine had condemned kidnappers to fight as

gladiators, and in AD 330 he allowed a *munus* (which included both theatrical displays and gladiatorial combats) to be given at Hispalum in Umbria (Italy) as part of celebrations for the cult of the imperial house. There is firm evidence for gladiatorial combat continuing into the fifth century AD in Rome, although the spectacles were not as lavish or as common as in earlier centuries. When Flavius Symmachus was Urban Prefect, barbarian captives were forced to fight both gladiators and wild beasts in the arena (AD 383-4). However, it is clear that the cost of putting on spectacles was escalating and other legislation limited senatorial expenditure on both theatrical and gladiatorial spectacles.

Commemorative medallions (*contorniates*) of Valentinian III (AD 419-455) with depictions of gladiatorial combat on their reverse demonstrate that such displays continued in Rome into the fifth century. One of the last documentary references to gladiators is in AD 404 when a monk, Telemachus, was torn apart by an irate crowd when he tried to stop a *munus* in Rome, inadvertently becoming part of the spectacle himself.

Outside Rome, gladiatorial shows are not mentioned in the literary sources after Arcadius (AD 383-408). Perhaps by this time Christian disapproval was beginning to have an effect, coupled with economic factors. In the western provinces, evidence for gladiatorial shows is sparse after the third century AD. It may also be that there was no longer the same incentive for individuals to fight as gladiators. In the eastern provinces the evidence suggests that gladiatorial games became rare after the mid-/late fourth century; they are not mentioned after the reign of Arcadius, and there is no mention of them at all at Constantinople. By the mid-fifth century Christian writers were criticising other forms of spectacle without mentioning gladiators. However, animal displays continued to entertain mass audiences.

Animal shows

Always popular, *venationes* continued as a characteristic feature of games celebrated at provincial capitals in honour of emperors, but they were evidently increasingly expensive. Any local officials who wanted to stage such spectacles, through choice or in connection with public office, had to make considerable monetary outlay. Thus at the beginning of the fifth century AD Symmachus' frustration and anger is understandable when he writes to the sons of Nicomarchus: 'We intended to retain the crocodiles advertised for the theatrical spectacle until your arrival, but they, having persevered in their hunger strike, which was emaciating them for fifty days at a stretch, were killed in the combat in the second games. We will preserve the two that are still alive now until your arrival, although there

23. Diptych of Areobindus, AD 506.

is no guarantee that they will be able to live long because they are refusing
food' (*Letters* 6.43).

By late antiquity there were a number of changes in the nature of animal
displays. Exotic animals no longer had the crowd-pull they once enjoyed,
mainly because there were few exotic animals which were still to be seen
or available *en masse*. There were still combats, but they often included
the use of props which effectively turned the tables on the human com-

24. Diptych of Anastasius, AD 517.

batants because they provoked and enraged the animals, increasing the human danger (and the entertainment value).

In this context a number of scenes depicted on consular diptychs are most informative. These were hinged, two-leaved, carved ivory plaques produced from the fourth to sixth centuries. They were connected with assumption of high office and were presumably bestowed as deluxe gifts. As such they have the advantage of being closely datable. Several of them show scenes of public spectacle, preserving a visual record of the games staged to celebrate consular appointment. On the Diptych of Areobindus (AD 506), below the main scene of the seated consul there is a composite picture of the games (Fig. 23). The majority of the animals shown are bears. One is depicted attacking a kind of oval cage in which a person's head is visible. This is possibly an *ericius*, as mentioned in a letter of Theodoric (Cassiodorus *Variae* 5.42) of the early sixth century AD; this would have provided some limited protection for the individual as it moved around the arena, rather like a very large hamster ball. Another bear has been injured on a spike extending from some kind of chest-piece worn by another man. Down to the right, a sort of dummy with a perforated head is shown; this is a *palea*, mentioned in the same letter of Theodoric, which could be used to taunt and excite the animals in a novel manner. There also seem to be contests between animals: a mule strikes a bear in the chest with its hind legs, and a lion and bull are in close combat. The public context of these displays is very clear, with the heads of the audience filling the top two corners. On a slightly later diptych of

25. Stadium, Aphrodisias (Turkey). Originally constructed in the late first century AD to accommodate a variety of spectacles, the east end (in foreground) was modified in late antiquity by the insertion of a small arena.

Anastasius (AD 517), at one side there are scenes of acrobats, and of bears fighting. A nearby contraption has two men in baskets apparently suspended by ropes held by them from a large timber upright. Below them a bear appears to be licking his lips (Fig. 24)! On the other side there are similar scenes, but also several instances of the *cochlea* (literally snail), a kind of revolving door behind which a man shelters, clearly intended to drive the animal into a frenzy in its attempts to get at him. Such a mechanism is also shown on an intriguing third-century AD relief from Sofia (Bulgaria).

The venues for animal displays in Rome had been the amphitheatre and, possibly more frequently, the Circus Maximus. In Constantinople it was the circus or another building called the *kynegion*, a structure shaped like an amphitheatre but exclusively for *venationes*. It is here that the last recorded instance of animal displays took place in Constantinople on 1 January 537 during consular games. The type of modification seen in the stadium at Aphrodisias (Fig. 25) as well as the stadium at Athens and the circus at Jerash (Jordan) may have been carried out to accommodate such spectacles.

Aquatic displays
With the exception of Philip the Arab's display, held in the middle of the third century as part of Rome's 1000th birthday celebrations, *naumachiae* did not continue in Rome after the early second century AD. However, an

interesting phenomenon of late antiquity, particularly in the eastern provinces, is the number of structures, notably theatres, that were adapted to accommodate water displays. The theatre at Argos, already modified once to a more Roman design, was further altered with the addition of a wall around the orchestra at the level of the fifth row of seats. An aqueduct provided the means to flood the resultant arena. Sometime before AD 400, the entire orchestra of the odeion at Ptolemais (Libya), a small structure which had originally served as a council meeting room (*bouleuterion*), was waterproofed to serve as a tank for aquatic displays. The area was restrictive, 7.5 metres in diameter and 1.3 metres deep. Similar modifications occurred in the theatres at Paphos (Cyprus), Corinth and Athens, and many more. The size of the area would have limited the type of display, and perhaps a Roman version of synchronised swimming was envisaged, along the lines of the Ziegfeld Follies of the early twentieth century. Given that most of these late examples occur in the eastern Mediterranean (a notable western exception is the theatre at Ostia), modifications may have been linked to the notorious Maiuma festivals. Probably of Phoenician origin, the Maiuma gained a reputation by the late empire for aquatic, candle-lit nocturnal activities by scantily clad female performers.

Chariot racing

Of all the Roman spectacles, chariot racing is the most closely associated with the Byzantine world. Although circus spectacles were not as common as in the West until the third century, they became particularly popular in the East later on, focussing imperial ceremony and patronage, and popular enthusiasm, as the circus became a primary location of interaction between ruler and ruled. The most lavish and important games were those associated with anniversaries of imperial births, victories, and other state and political occasions. By this time the physical relationship between circus and imperial palace had been set. The Palatine imperial palace in Rome overlooked the Circus Maximus and this relationship was drawn on for the new regional capitals of the Tetrarchy, instituted by Diocletian in AD 293. This was the place where the emperor encountered and showed himself to his subjects. This physical proximity is evident in Constantinople and was depicted on the base-reliefs of the Theodosian obelisk placed on the central barrier of the circus. The emperor is shown in the *kathisma* or imperial box. The obelisk itself, placed on the spina by Theodosius I at the end of the fourth century, again mirrors earlier practice, copying the obelisks of Augustus and Constantius II in the Circus Maximus.

As the popularity of chariot racing increased in late antiquity, so feelings could run high amongst the spectators. Ammianus Marcellinus mocked race fans who argued that the state itself would fall unless their favoured team exited first from the starting gates and properly negotiated the turns. He wrote that 'their temple, their dwelling, their assembly and the height of all their hopes is the Circus Maximus' (37.4.28-31). A riot took place in AD 390 at Thessaloniki over the imprisonment of a favourite charioteer. The emperor Theodosius retaliated by enticing people into the circus for games and then sending in troops who killed between 7,000 and 15,000 people. Such violence is often blamed on the circus factions. By the fifth century AD the range of colours had been subsumed into the Blues and the Greens, and these were complex organisations which not only provided stabling, chariots, drivers and training as of old, but also the animals for circus intervals and the entertainers, such as the dancers and musicians figured on the Theodosian obelisk base. Epigraphic evidence from Aphrodisias demonstrates that they were also involved in theatrical productions. It is tempting to think of the factions in the fifth and sixth centuries as rowdy, quasi-political bodies waiting for the next race-day to cause problems. In fact there was very little trouble in the circus before the fifth century whereas there are a good number of documented cases of riots and rowdiness in the theatre. The circus had a much bigger area, and factions within the audience were much more visible in their colours, akin to stands of football supporters today. The most famous of the circus riots in late antiquity are the so-called 'Nike' Riots in Constantinople (AD 532), a factional dispute that had little direct concern with actual chariot racing but which threatened to replace the emperor Justinian and the suppression of which resulted in 30,000 deaths.

The huge popularity, not only of chariot racing, but also of the chari-oteers themselves at this time, is illustrated by the career of Porphyrius (late fifth to early sixth century AD). Seven statues to Porphyrius were set up on the *spina* of the circus in Constantinople; the bases of only two survive and are now in the Istanbul Archaeological Museum. They were set up by the Greens and the Blues; he raced for both of them in a career during which he came back from retirement several times. As well as praising Porphyrius, the epigrams also record the names of successful horses.

As, one by one, the great metropoleis of the Roman world were lost (e.g. Carthage, Alexandria) so chariot racing disappeared. The very last chariot races in the Circus Maximus were staged by the Ostrogothic King Totila in AD 550 (Procopius, *Gothic Wars* 3.37.4) . As we have seen, chariot racing did remain a key part of imperial ceremonial in the circus of Constantinople as late as the twelfth century, but by that time it was a shadow of its former self.

Chapter 7

Roman Spectacle: Ancient Contexts and Modern Perceptions

Although the *ludi* (the theatrical and circus games) and the *munera* (the gladiatorial games) had very different origins, the political advantage to be gained from such displays had been well-recognised in Rome during the last two centuries BC. In the imperial period it was common practice for the emperor to put on special games to commemorate victories and anniversaries, and it was an accepted obligation of members of the provincial elites to present spectacles for public entertainment at their own expense, following the ideal of enhancing the life of the community ('euergetism'). Indeed, it was often a requirement of those holding public office. These games could be very elaborate, involving a broad range of different types of display, sometimes over several days. Epigraphic evidence indicates that such obligatory shows were given in Italy and the provinces by such individuals to preserve their memory, but effectively they were also a tax on status, while the donor's reputation (*famia*) was greatly enhanced as a result. Thus public entertainment provided a focal point for the exercise of power at different levels.

The modern view of these spectacles is often to separate them, but in reality they frequently overlapped. One set of games could include a wide variety of different types of entertainment, sometimes using the same venue (such as the Colosseum with gladiatorial combat and wild beast hunts), sometimes using multiple locations. Nevertheless, they all formed part of the same celebration.

The important link between spectacle and political power is at no time more obvious than in the first century BC, with the manoeuvrings of figures such as Julius Caesar and Pompey. They and their contemporaries were caught up in an inflationary spiral of competition, as each man aimed to outdo his rivals. Early in his career, as *aedile* in 65 BC, Caesar arranged a number of different displays, including wild animal hunts and theatrical performances. He also arranged for a gladiatorial *munus*, but according to Suetonius (*Julius* 10) it involved fewer pairs of gladiators than he had originally planned. Apparently the group he had hired was so large that it

26. Tombstone of the Thracian gladiator Marcus
Antonius Exochus, who fought under Trajan (*CIL*
6.10194, now lost).

terrified his political enemies, and emergency legislation was passed to
restrict the number of gladiators that anyone could keep in Rome. Even
so, there were still 320 pairs (Pliny, *Natural History* 33.53; Plutarch,
Caesar 5). No specific venues are mentioned in any account, although the
gladiatorial combat presumably took place in the Forum Romanum.

Pompey responded by providing Rome with her first permanent theatre, which he dedicated in 55 BC with lavish entertainments. These
included music and gymnastic contests, a horse-race in the circus and

animal displays which resulted in large-scale slaughter. Dio (39.38.2) reported that 500 lions were used up in five days, and eighteen elephants fought against men in heavy armour.

This practice of variety continued into the imperial period. The tombstone of Marcus Antonius Exochus (*CIL* 6.10194) (Fig. 26), a Thracian gladiator, refers to the games Trajan held to celebrate his Dacian triumph in the early second century AD. Exochus fought several times, once receiving *missio* and once being victorious. The *Fasti Ostienses* imply that these games were in fact spread over several years culminating in AD 109 when nearly 10,000 gladiators were involved and sea-battles were staged in Trajan's *naumachia*.

Evidence from outside Rome indicates that the same variety was a feature of shows in Italy and the provinces. A marble relief panel from the tomb of the *duovir* N. Clovatius at Pompeii provides a permanent record laid out in three superimposed registers of a set of games involving both gladiators and animal displays. The event opened with a parade (*pompa*) of gladiators led by trumpeters (*tubicines*). Gladiators are shown arming, then in combat. In the lower register are various animal combat scenes. A similar variety is displayed on the Zliten mosaic.

At Allifae in Italy, the *duovir* Lucius Fadius gave lavish spectacles in connection with the imperial cult to mark his election in the second half of the first century AD (*CIL* 9.2350). He exhibited 30 pairs of gladiators and a hunt of African beasts; a few months later, with a contribution of 13,000 sesterces from the town council, he staged a hunt and displayed 21 pairs of gladiators. After he had completed his year of office, he paid for theatrical shows out of his own wealth. This was an individual who maximised the personal benefit to be accrued from his public service.

By the later second century a debate in the senate over the level of expenditure for shows resulted in legislation which included a ranking of gladiators by price and experience, and matching them with the quality of *munus* that a local magistrate was required to fund (Fig. 27). There has been much debate over the precise meaning and details of this law, but there can be little doubt of the organisation involved and wealth expended on a yearly basis to provide gladiatorial *munera* across the Roman world. The provision of the gladiatorial performers may have been through provincial *ludi* maintained by the emperor which are attested across the empire. This legislation also gives important insights into gladiatorial hierarchies, hinted at in other evidence. Moreover, single combat, whilst possibly the norm, was not the only way for gladiators to appear in the arena; they could also make up battle groups (as *gregarii*).

By the mid first century AD a day at the games would comprise animal

Type/grade	Amount (*sestertii*)	Amount (modern estimate)
munera assiforana (profit-making gladiatorial combats)	less than 30,000	£200,000
Class IV	30,000-60,000	£200,000-£400,000
Class III	60,000-100,000	£400,000-£650,000
Class II	100,000-150,000	£650,000- £1,000,000
Class I	150,000-200,000 & above	£1-1.2 million

At least half the total number of gladiators must be *gregarii* at a cost of 1,000-2,000 *sestertii*.
Damnati ad bestias were available at a cost of 600 *sestertii*.
Special Celtic sacrificial victims (*trinquii:* perhaps a special type of *bestiarius*) were available as substitutes for gladiators at 2,000 *sestertii*.

27. Provisions of a *senatus consultum de pretiis gladiatorum minuendis* (*CIL* 2.6278) issued AD 177-180 to regulate the prices of gladiators sold to organisers of games. Modern estimates are based on D. Bomgardner, *The Story of the Roman Amphitheatre*, London 2000.

displays in the morning, with executions over lunchtime (*ludi meridiani*) as the appetiser to the main course of gladiatorial combat in the afternoon. Seneca, in a letter to his friend Lucilius (*Letters* 7), bemoaned the fact that he had gone to the arena at midday 'hoping for a little wit and humour', only to be confronted by 'butchery', claiming 'then [i.e. in the morning] men were thrown to lions and bears, but at midday to the audience'. Interestingly, Seneca appreciated the gladiatorial games for their educational value, as a demonstration of moral excellence (*virtus*). Pliny the Younger, in his panegyric of Trajan, referred to a 'beautiful' show where the detested informers were publicly degraded and punished (*Panegyric* 34.3). Public execution was obviously a very powerful judicial retribution and deterrent, but for a society so much defined by status, it was also humiliating. Convicted criminals served an exemplary purpose for the public good. According to the legislation published under Marcus Aurelius (Fig. 27), it was possible to purchase criminals who had been condemned *ad bestias* for execution in privately funded displays. It was perhaps by this means that Marcus Putilius Macedon was able to include four convicts (*noxii*) in his 'magnificent four-day show' at Beneventum (*CIL* 9.2237), which also included four wild animals (*ferae*) and sixteen bears. These games give an idea of the relative scale of such games outside the capital.

The public aspect of execution is not that unfamiliar in more recent historical times, when public hangings would be anticipated and enjoyed with a picnic. However, Roman executions went one stage further, sometimes being dressed up with a mythological or ethnographic elaboration. Strabo (*Geography* 6.2) witnessed the execution of the Sicilian bandit Selurus who had been sent to Rome to suffer his fate. The setting not only aimed to recall his criminal stomping ground (Mount Etna), but also his nickname:

> ... a certain Selurus, called 'son of Aetna', was sent up to Rome because he had put himself at the head of an army and for a long time had overrun the region around Aetna with frequent raids. I saw him torn to pieces by wild beasts ... in the Forum, for he was placed on a lofty platform as though on Aetna, which was made suddenly to break up and collapse, and he was carried down into cages of wild beasts, fragile cages that had been prepared beneath the platform for that purpose.

From a spectator's point of view, the anticipation and tension must have been exhilarating.

The *damnati* were condemned criminals or people enslaved in war. By watching their deaths, metropolitan spectators were witnessing and endorsing the course of justice. There were three main methods of execution in the arena: burning alive (*crematio*), throwing to the beasts (*ad bestias*), and crucifixion. Thus, Christians were famously burned by Nero in the Circus, as well as hunted by animals and crucified after the great fire of AD 64 (Tacitus, *Annals* 15.44). An advertisement for games at Pompeii (*CIL* IV 9983a) included criminals to be crucified in the amphitheatre during a regular *munus*. However, crucifixion was slow and boring with little spectator appeal. If it was combined with other instruments of execution, for example animals, then it was more interesting. This is certainly the case with Blandina, a Christian woman who was martyred at Lyon in AD 177; she was hung upside down on a post as bait for animals.

None of these displays offered any realistic chance of survival, as compared with those condemned to fight as gladiators or *venatores*. A mythological setting might be provided, as is clearly referred to by Martial in his account of the games for the inauguration of the Colosseum. For example, the story of Orpheus, who charmed the animals with his music, was re-enacted – except that he was actually torn apart by the animals. Another involved some kind of re-enactment of the encounter between Pasiphae and the bull (the offspring of which was the Minotaur).

The Zliten mosaic depicts several executions (Fig. 28). Criminals are shown tied to miniature chariots and wheeled up by attendants to be

28. Detail of scenes from the Zliten mosaic, showing a fight between a chained bear and bull and condemned criminals being thrown to the beasts.

attacked by wild animals, some of which are urged on by whips. Another North African mosaic from El Djem (Tunisia) shows leopards and bears within a bloodstained arena. The deaths of the condemned men, hands bound behind their backs as they are attacked by animals, are shown in grisly and graphic detail. The incorporation of such scenes into interior decoration was a way for the elite to align themselves with the very visible administration of justice and provide a reminder to the viewer of the natural order of the Roman world.

Further social reinforcement occurred during spectator engagement with the venues themselves. From the second century BC, the seating arrangements in the theatre came to reflect and reaffirm the social hierarchy, at least in Rome. To some extent this also became true for the amphitheatre also. The evidence is fragmentary and has to be gleaned from epigraphic and literary sources. The senate sat separately for the first time at Roman games in 194 BC (Livy 34.54). In 67 BC the *lex Roscia* reserved the first 14 rows of seats for equestrians (Cicero, *To Atticus* 2.29.3). This was renewed and reinforced under Augustus with his *lex Iulia theatralis* (Suetonius, *Augustus* 44) which demanded the audience be seated in a hierarchical fashion by social rank and gender. Similar segregation in the Colosseum is confirmed by the divisions in the *cavea* and by inscriptions on the seats. The most dramatic division is the separation of the upper two tiers from the rest; a vertical drop of 5 metres kept non-citizens, women and slaves well away from the rest of the audience (Fig. 31). Access to these seats further emphasised this segregation as different entrances needed to be used depending on where a spectator was seated. The only women to enjoy ringside seats were the Vestal Virgins and members of the imperial family. Formal segregation was less rigid in the circus. A senatorial resolution reserved the first row of seats for senators (Suetonius, *Augustus* 44.1). By the middle of the first century AD equestrians were given a fixed area of seating (Tacitus, *Annals* 15.32). In stark contrast to the theatre and amphitheatre, there does not seem to have been any attempt to separate male and female spectators in the circus. The concept of seating arrangements reflecting social rank was certainly adopted in theatres in towns in Italy and the provinces where epigraphic evidence suggests, for example, that there were special seats reserved for priests.

The spectacle arenas of the Roman world were undoubtedly a theatre of death, but one in which the urban population experienced the patronage of emperors and elites, the dominance of the Roman world over the barbarian, the superiority of urban civilisation over the raw forces of nature, and of the forces of order and justice over transgression and criminality. Modern observers have been disturbed by the success and popularity of the Roman spectacles. But the disquiet is all the deeper because contemporary sports media and other entertainments harmonise so well with the raw enjoyment of the Roman audience.

And what of any residual influence of these spectacles? There are many instances which can be cited since the Roman period of single combat, animal displays and fights and other forms of potentialy life-threatening competition on public show. Itinerant circus troupes with trained animal acts, bear-baiting and cock-fighting were familiar features of the medieval and later periods. The collection and display of exotic animals as an expression of power over both the human and natural worlds was a custom followed by Lorenzo the Magnificent in fifteenth-century Florence; the gift of a giraffe from Qaitbay, the Sultan of Egypt, honoured him as a Prince as opposed to a merchant. Flora and fauna from Europe and further afield were part of a grand procession through Paris in 1798 extolling the triumphs of Napoleon. In the twentieth century panda diplomacy (continuing a practice dating back to the Tang dynasty in the seventh century AD) resulted in China presenting 23 giant pandas as diplomatic gifts to nine different countries. Many of the world's great zoos originated as displays of imperial power overseas.

In the Californian Gold Rush of 1849, as cock and dog fights became tame entertainments for the hardened and desperate miners, grizzly bears were captured (no mean feat in itself) and pitched against bulls in a circular arena surrounded by seats. There were often protests at the way the bulls' horns were sawn off, reducing their fighting effectiveness; they wanted a good, fair fight, even though death was inevitable for one of the animals.

The Spanish bullfight (the *corrida*) is often put forward as the closest modern equivalent to the Roman *venatio*, although no direct link has been proved. The colourful and showy costumes, the exaggerated and stylised postures of the human performers, the cult status of the matadors, all find parallels in the Roman world. Interestingly, in some places (such as the south of France) Roman amphitheatres are used for these spectacles, just as the stadium at Ephesus is used for camel wrestling.

It is much more difficult to produce equivalent examples involving human combatants. Boxing, bare-knuckle fighting and modern cage-fighting come closest in terms of danger of death, while the huge following that professional wrestling has, particularly in North America and Mexico, emphasises the showmanship and celebrity status of the performers.

From its outset the Hollywood film industry latched on to the excitement of Roman spectacle, from the heydey of the sword and sandal film, including spectacles in Delmer Daves's *Demetrius and the Gladiators* (1954), William Wyler's *Ben Hur* (1959), Stanley Kubrick's *Spartacus* (1960), and Anthony Mann's *Fall of the Roman Empire* (1964), to the modern revival centred around Ridley Scott's *Gladiator* (2000) and HBO's television success *Rome* (2005-7). All such productions heavily emphasised the bloodlust, cruelty and 'uncivilised' nature of Roman culture, with strong moralising and eroticising elements.

Appendix

Roman Buildings for Spectacle

Circus

Typical plan: Less architecturally formalised in the republic, by the early imperial period the circus had a hairpin plan, with the seating on vaulted substructures. The race-track had a central barrier (usually referred to as the *spina*), around which the competitors raced; this was often ornamented with statues, fountains and lap-counting devices. At the opposite end to the curved end there were starting gates (*carceres*), the mechanism of which has been reconstructed from the evidence surviving in the circus at Lepcis Magna, and from comparative iconography. The track of the Roman circus was usually at least 400 metres in length (the Circus Maximus was approximately 540 metres).

Types of associated entertainment: primarily chariot and horse racing, with a wide range of interval entertainments (including *venationes*, athletics, dancing).

Good surviving examples: because of their great size, circuses are often less well-preserved than other entertainment buildings.

- Circus Maximus, Rome. Traditionally first established under the kings, it reached its final form in the period of Trajan. Largest circus of the Roman world with two red granite obelisks on the spina (Fig. 29).
- Lepcis Magna, western Libya (mid second century AD). Located immediately adjacent to the earlier amphitheatre, forming an impressive entertainment complex.
- Tarragona, north-east Spain (Domitianic). Built in association with imperial cult games in the heart of the city. Substructures survive in the cellars of a number of later buildings, some of which have been excavated and can be visited.
- Tyre, Lebanon (late second/early third century AD). One of the best preserved Roman circuses. The track is approximately 450 metres long. Seating was supported on vaulted substructures and a red granite obelisk stood on the central *spina*.
- Constantinople, north-west Turkey (Severan foundation, fourth/fifth century AD restructuring). Massive surviving substructures at the curved end. Several monuments remain standing on the *spina*.

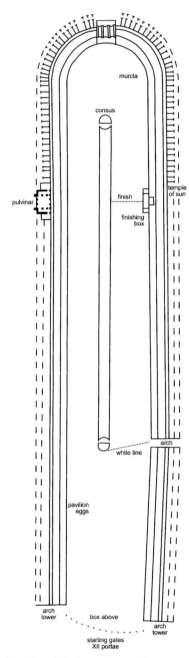

29. Circus Maximus, Rome. Plan.

Theatre

Typical plan: Usually semi-circular or D-shaped in plan with an elaborate stage building. Advances in building technology allowed Roman theatres to be constructed on flat ground using vaulted substructures to support the seating. Found in cities across the empire and also associated with religious sanctuaries in the countryside.

Types of associated entertainment: Dramatic performances. By the imperial period performances were predominantly low-grade performances such as mimes, pantomimes and farces, though there is evidence for the continuation of drama. In the eastern provinces, theatres were often remodelled to allow for the accommodation of gladiatorial games, animal displays and other kinds of spectacle. The details of modification can vary considerably.

Good surviving examples:

- Orange, southern France (later first century AD), which has surviving corbels to support awnings for the stage-building (Fig. 30).
- Aspendos, southern Turkey (mid-second century AD). Surviving corbels on exterior of *cavea* for awnings.
- Bostra, southern Syria (second century AD). Built up entirely on vaulted substructures and survives to its full original height.
- Lepcis Magna, Libya (AD 1-2). Built up on vaulted substructures. Epigraphic dedications survive *in situ*.

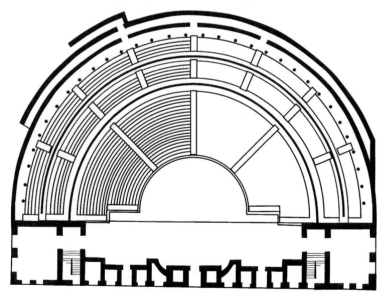

30. Theatre, Orange (France), late first century AD. Plan.

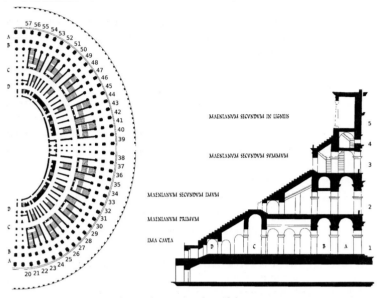

31. Colosseum, Rome. Plan and cross-section of the *cavea*.

Ampthitheatre

Typical plan: Usually elliptical rather than circular in plan with an oval arena, completely surrounded by seating. It is a structure exclusively associated with the Romans. There are well over 200 amphitheatres known across the Roman world, predominantly in Italy, North Africa and the western provinces. Fewer are known from the East, although our knowledge is always changing.

Types of associated entertainment: Gladiatorial, animal and hunting displays. Occasionally water displays.

Good surviving examples:

- Pompeii (70-65 BC). Earliest surviving, datable permanent amphitheatre, with seating on solid substructures with external staircases.
- Colosseum, Rome (inaugurated AD 80). Properly known as the Flavian Amphitheatre, the largest amphitheatre of the Roman World (Fig. 30). Arena with extensive subterranean structures, seating on concrete vaulting. External crowd control barriers and corbels for awnings (Fig. 31).
- El Djem, Tunisia (first half third century AD). Seating entirely on vaulted stone and mortared rubble substructures. Subterranean rooms beneath the central arena.
- Nimes, southern France (later first century AD). Two-storeyed façade with surviving exterior corbels for awnings (Fig. 11). Vaulted stone substructures for seating.

- Pergamum, north-western Turkey (second/third century AD). Built in a narrow stream valley which partly supports the structure, supplemented by mortared rubble vaulting (Fig. 12).

Stadium

Typical plan: usually hairpin shaped in plan, overall 200-230 metres in length. Rare in the Roman West, but common in the eastern provinces.

Types of associated entertainment: primarily athletics, but in the East stadia were often modified to accommodate gladiatorial and animal displays.

Good surviving examples:

- Stadium of Domitian, Rome (dedicated AD 86). Located on the Campus Martius, with an overall length of 275 metres. Seating supported on vaulted substructures with the track dictating the shape and size of the modern Piazza Navona. Paired with Domitian's *odeum*.
- Perge, southern Turkey (second century AD). A well-preserved example built throughout of stone ashlar masonry. Subsequently modified with the insertion of a walled arena at the curved end.
- Aphrodisias, western Turkey (later first century AD). One of three known examples in Greece and Asia Minor which are curved at both ends (with Nicopolis in north-western Greece, and Laodiceia ad Lycum in western Turkey). Length of 270 metres, and built from the outset to accommodate a range of spectacles and entertainments. Subsequently modified with the insertion of a walled arena at the curved end (Fig. 25).

Naumachia

An artificial basin constructed for large-scale aquatic displays, also referred to as a *stagnum*. The term *naumachia* transferred to the spectacles themselves, particularly the sea battle re-enactments. These purpose-built structures were a particular phenomenon of the capital.

Types of associated entertainment: Sea-battle re-enactments and other aquatic displays involving both human and animal performers.

Examples: There are no well-preserved examples.

- Stagnum of Augustus, Rome (late first century BC). Built in the Transtiber region by Augustus and later used by Titus. No visible remains (Fig. 19).
- Naumachia of Trajan, Rome (inaugurated AD 109). Built in the Prati di Castello area of Rome. Antiquarian views and plans, and some excavated remains (Fig. 20).

Further Reading

The amount of material published particularly in the last ten years on the subject of Roman spectacle is enormous, and it can vary considerably in treatment and quality. This list represents some of the most important publications; all have extensive bibliographies of their own.

General
R. Auguet, *Cruelty and Civilisation*, London 1994; A. Futrell, *The Roman Games,* Oxford 2006; E. Köhne and C. Ewigleben (eds), *Gladiators and Caesars. The Power of Spectacle in Ancient Rome*, London 2000; D.G. Kyle, *Spectacles of Death in Ancient Rome*, London 1998; A. La Regina, *Sangue e Arena*, Catalogue of an exhibition held at the Colosseum, Rome, 22 June 2001-7 Jan. 2002, Milan 2001; P. Plass, *The Game of Death in Ancient Rome, Arena Sport and Political Suicide*, Wisconsin 1995; D. Potter, 'Entertainers in the Roman Empire', in D.S. Potter and D.J. Mattingly (ed.), *Life, Death and Entertainment in the Roman Empire*, Ann Arbor 1999, 256-325; T. Wiedemann, *Emperors and Gladiators*, London 1992; M. Wistrand, *Entertainment and Violence in Ancient Rome*, Göteborg 1992.

Venues
General coverage: A.J. Brothers, 'Buildings for Entertainment', in I.M. Barton (ed.), *Roman Public Buildings*, Exeter 1989, 97-125; H. Dodge, 'Amusing the Masses: Buildings for Entertainment and Leisure in the Roman World', in D.S. Potter and D.J. Mattingly (ed.), *Life, Death and Entertainment in the Roman Empire*, Ann Arbor 1999, 205-55.
More specific treatments: D. Bomgardner, *The Story of the Roman Amphitheatre*, London 2000 (particular reference to North African material); A. Gabucci (ed.), *The Colosseum*, tr. M. Becker, Los Angeles 2001; J.-C. Golvin, *L'amphithéâtre romain. Essai sur la théorisation de sa forme et ses fonctions* (2 vols), Paris 1988; F. Sear, *Roman Theatres. An Architectural Study*, Oxford Monographs on Classical Archaeology, Oxford 2006;

J. Humphrey, *Roman Circuses*, London 1986 (still the standard work); J. Nelis-Clément and J.-M. Roddaz (ed.), *Le Cirque Romain et son Image*, Bordeaux 2008 (this includes articles on the structures themselves, including the recently discovered circus at Colchester and circus games iconography); K. Welch, *The Roman Amphitheatre from its Origins to the Colosseum*, Cambridge 2007; T. Wilmott, *The Roman Amphithitheatre in Britain*, Stroud 2008; T. Wilmott (ed.), *Roman Amphitheatres and* Spectacula: *a 21st-century Perspective*, Oxford 2009 (articles on the structures, including the recently discovered and excavated amphitheatre at Serdica, gladiatorial identity, the Magerius mosaic, gladiatorial graffiti and the Ephesus gladiators).

Gladiators, gladiatorial and animal displays
R. Dunkle, *Gladiators. Violence and Spectacle in Ancient Rome*, Harlow 2008; L. Jacobelli, *Gladiators at Pompeii*, trans. M. Becker, Los Angeles 2003; G. Jennison, *Animals for Show and Pleasure in Ancient Rome*, Manchester 1937 (repr. Philadelphia 1961); M. Junkelmann, *Das Spiel mit dem Tod. So kämpften Roms Gladiatoren*, Mainz 2000
On the Ephesus gladiators, Kanz and Grossschmidt in Wilmott 2009 (above).
For the Pompeian gladiatorial graffiti: A.E. Cooley and M.G.L. Cooley, *Pompeii: A Sourcebook*, London 2004.

Horse racing and chariot racing
A. Cameron, *Porphyrios the Charioteer*, Oxford 1972; A. Cameron, *Circus Factions, Blues and Greens at Rome and Byzantium*, Oxford 1978; C. Landes (ed.), *Le cirque et les courses de char, Rome-Byzance*, Lattes 1990.

Naumachiae and aquatic displays
G. Cariou, *La Naumachie. Morituri te Salutant*, Paris 2009; K. Coleman, 'Launching into History: Aquatic Displays in the Early Empire', *Journal of Roman Studies* 83 (1993), 48-74; F. Garello, 'Sport or ShowBiz? The *naumachiae* of Imperial Rome', in S. Bell and G. Davies (eds), *Games and Festivals in Classical Antiquity* (BAR Int. Ser. 1220) Oxford 2004, 115-24.

Spectacle in Rome
R.C. Beacham, *Spectacle Entertainments of Early Imperial Rome*, New Haven 1999; K. Coleman, 'Entertaining Rome', in J.C. Coulston and H. Dodge (eds), *Ancient Rome: The Archaeology of the Eternal City*, Oxford University School of Archaeology Monograph 54, Oxford 2000, 210-58;

P. Connolly, *Colosseum: Rome's Arena of Death*, London 2003; K. Hopkins and M. Beard, *The Colosseum*, London 2005; R. Rea (ed.), *Anfiteatro Flavio. Immagine testimonianze spettacoli*, Rome 1988.

Spectacle in Italy and the western provinces
J.M. Alvarez Martínez and J.J. Enríquez Navascués (ed.), *El Anfiteatro en la Hispania Romana. Coloquio Internacional Mérida, 26-28 Noviembre 1992*, Mérida 1994; P. del Castillo, L.A. De Cuenca and *El Circo en Hispania Romana*, Mérida 2001; C.-L Domergue, C. Landes and J.-M. Pailler (eds), *Spectacula I. Gladiateurs et Amphithéâtres,* Lattes 1990.
Inscriptions relating to gladiators, gladiatorial and other arena displays from Rome, Italy and the Western Empire are collected together in a seven-volume work: *Epigrafia anfiteatrale dell'occidente romano*, Rome. 1. *Roma*, 1988; 2. *Regiones Italiae VI-XI*, 1989; 3. *Regiones Italiae II-V, Sicilia, Sardinia et Corsica*, 1992; 4. *Regio Italiae I: Latium*, 1996; 5. *Alpes Maritimae, Gallia Narbonensis, Tres Galliae, Germaniae, Britannia*, 2000; 6. *Roma: anfiteatri e strutture annese con una nuova edizione e commento delle iscrizioni del Colosseo*, 2004; 7. *Baetica,Tarraconensis, Lusitania*, 2009.

Spectacle in the eastern provinces
The classic treatment of the primary evidence is still L. Robert, *Les Gladiateurs dans l'Orient Grec*, Paris 1940. More recent works include: M. Carter, 'Gladiators and Monomachoi: Greek Attitudes to a Roman "Cultural Performance"', *International Journal of the History of Sport*, 26:2 (2009), 298-322; H. Dodge, 'Circuses in the Roman East: a Reappraisal', in J. Nelis-Clément and J.-M. Roddaz (eds), *Le Cirque Romain et Son Image*, Bordeaux 2008, 133-46; H. Dodge, 'Amphitheatres in the Roman East', in T. Wilmott (ed.), *Roman Amphitheatres and* Spectacula*: a 21st-century Perspective*, Oxford 2009, 29-46; C. Mann, 'Gladiators in the Greek East: A Case Study in Romanization', *International Journal of the History of Sport*, 26:2 (2009), 272-97; C. Roueché, *Performers and Partisans*, London 1993; Z. Weiss, 'Adopting a Novelty: the Jews and the Roman Games in Palestine', in J. Humphrey (ed.), *The Roman and Byzantine Near East: Some Recent Archaeological Research* , vol. 2, JRA Supplement Series 31, Portsmouth RI 1999, 23-49; K. Welch, 'The Stadium at Aphrodisias', *American Journal of Archaeology* 102 (1998), 547-69.
For the depiction of spectacle in North African moaics: K. Dunbabin, *The Mosaics of Roman North Africa: Studies in Iconography and Patronage*, Oxford 1978, in particular chs 4 and 6.

Spectacle in late antiquity

R.F. Devoe, *Christianity and the Roman Games*, Philadelphia 2002; P. Veyne, 'Païens et chrétiens devant la gladiature', *Mélanges de l'École française de Rome: Antiquité* 111 (1999), 883-917; G. Ville, 'Les jeux de gladiateurs dans l'empire Chrétien', *Mélanges de l'École française de Rome: Antiquité* 72 (1960), 273-335.

The site of Aphrodisias has proved to be very important for spectacle in general, but in particular for entertainments in late antiquity. See in particular for the theatre: R.R.R. Smith and K.T. Erim (eds), *Aphrodisias Papers 2. The Theatre, a Sculptor's Workshop, Philosophers, and Coin-types*, Journal of Roman Archaeology Supp. 2, Ann Arbor, 1991.

For the spectacles depicted on consular diptychs: C. Olovsdotter, *The Consular Image: An Iconographical Study of the Consular Diptychs*, Oxford 2005.

Society and spectacle

K. Coleman, 'Fatal Charades: Roman Executions staged as Mythological Enactments', *Journal of Roman Studies* 80 (1990), 44-73; C. Edwards, *The Politics of Immorality in Ancient Rome*, Cambridge 1993.

On seating according to social order: J. Edmonson, 'Public Spectacles and Roman Social Relations', in T. Nogales Basarrate & A. Castellanos (eds), *Ludi Romani: Espectáculos en Hispania Romana*. Madrid, 2002, 21-43; E. Rawson, '*Discrimina Ordinum*, The Lex Julia Theatralis', *Papers of the British School at Rome* 55 (1987), 83-114.

On costs and expenditure: M. Carter, 'Gladiatorial Ranking and the "SC de Pretiis Gladiatorum Minuendis" (*CIL* II 6278 = *ILS* 5163)', *Phoenix* 57 (2003), 83-114; R. Duncan-Jones, *The Economy of the Roman Empire*, 2nd edn, London 1982.

Roman spectacle on film

M. Silveira Cyrino, *Big Screen Rome*, Oxford 2005; M. Winkler (ed.), *Gladiator: Film and History*, Oxford 2004; M. Winkler (ed.), *Spartacus: Film and History*, Oxford 2006.

Index

CLASSICAL
WORLD SERIES

RECENT TITLES IN THE SERIES
(for a full list see opposite title page)

Roman Frontiers in Britain
David J. Breeze

ISBN 978 1 85399 698 6

Hadrian's Wall and the Antonine Wall defined the far northern limits of the Roman Empire in Britain. Today, the spectacular remains of these great frontier works stand as mute testimony to one of the greatest empires the world has ever seen. This new accessible account, illustrated with 25 detailed photographs, maps and plans, describes the building of the Walls and reconstructs what life was like on the frontier. It places the Walls into their context both in Britain and in Europe, examining the development of Roman frontier installations over four centuries.

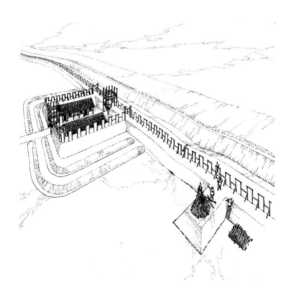

Cities of Roman Italy:
Pompeii, Herculaneum and Ostia
Guy de la Bédoyère

ISBN 978 1 85399 728 0

The ruins of Pompeii, Herculaneum, and Ostia have excited the imagination of scholars and tourists alike since early modern times. The removal of volcanic debris at Pompeii and Herculaneum, and the clearance of centuries of accumulated soil and vegetation from the ancient port city of Rome at Ostia, have provided us with the most important evidence for Roman urban life. Work goes on at all three sites to this day, and they continue to produce new surprises.

Pompeii is the subject of many accessible and useful books, but much less is available in English for the other two cities. This book is designed for students of classics and archaeology A-level or university courses who need a one-stop introduction to all three sites. Its principal focus is status and identity in Roman cities, and how these were expressed through institutions, public buildings and facilities, private houses and funerary monuments, against a backdrop of the history of the cities, their rise, their destruction, preservation and excavation.

The Plays of Aeschylus
A.F. Garvie

ISBN 978 1 85399 707 5

Aeschylus is the oldest of the three great Greek tragedians. Born probably in 525 or 524 BC, he lived through the end of tyranny at Athens and the restitution of democracy. He took part in the battle of Marathon in 490 and probably also in the battle of Salamis in 480, the subject of his *Persians*. During his life he made at least two visits to Sicily, and died there at Gela in 456 or 455.

This book deals with Aeschylus' six extant plays in the chronological order of their first production: *Persians*, the earliest Greek tragedy that has come down to us, *Seven against Thebes*, *Suppliants*, and the three plays of the *Oresteia* trilogy: *Agamemnon*, *Libation Bearers* and *Eumenides*. It also contains an essay on *Prometheus Bound*, now generally thought not to be by Aeschylus, but accepted as his in antiquity. The book is intended primarily as a readable introduction to the dramatist for A-level students of Classical Civilisation and Ancient History at school and in the first two years of university courses.

Greek Literature in the Roman Empire
Jason König

ISBN 978 1 85388 713 6

In this book Jason König offers for the first time an accessible yet comprehensive account of the multi-faceted Greek literature of the Roman Empire, focusing especially on the first three centuries AD. He covers in turn the Greek novels of this period, the satirical writing of Lucian, rhetoric, philosophy, scientific and miscellanistic writing, geography and history, biography and poetry, providing a vivid introduction to key texts with extensive quotation in translation. He also looks beyond the most commonly studied authors to reveal the full richness of this period's literature. The challenges and pleasures these texts offer to their readers have come to be newly appreciated in the classical scholarship of the last two or three decades. In addition there has been renewed interest in the role played by novelistic and rhetorical writing in the Greek culture of the Roman Empire more broadly, and in the many different ways in which these texts respond to the world around them. This volume offers a broad introduction to those exciting developments.

Athletics in the Ancient World
Zahra Newby

ISBN 978 1 85399 688 7

The athletic competitions that took place during festivals such as that at Olympia, or within the confines of city gymnasia, were a key feature of life in ancient Greece. From the commemoration of victorious athletes in poetry or sculpture to the archaeological remains of baths, gymnasia and stadia, surviving evidence offers plentiful testimony to the importance of athletic activity in Greek culture, and its survival well into Roman times.

This book offers an introduction to the many forms that athletics took in the ancient world, and to the sources of evidence by which we can study it. As well as looking at the role of athletics in archaic and classical Greece, it also covers the less-explored periods of the Hellenistic and Roman worlds. Many different aspects of athletics are considered – not only the well-known contests of athletic festivals, but also the place of athletic training within civic education and military training, and its integration into the bathing culture of the Roman world.